THE LEGAL ENTERPRISE

THE LEGAL ENTERPRISE

ROBERT E. RODES, Jr.
Professor of Law
Notre Dame Law School

National University Publications
KENNIKAT PRESS   //   1976
Port Washington, N. Y.   //   London
A DUNELLEN PUBLISHING COMPANY BOOK

Printed in the United States of America

Distributed in United States and Canada by
Kennikat Press, Port Washington, N. Y. 11050

Distributed in British Commonwealth (except Canada) by
Martin Robertson & Company Ltd., London

Library of Congress Cataloging in Publication Data

Rodes, Robert E
    The legal enterprise.

    (National university publications)
    Bibliography: p.
    1. Law—Philosophy. I. Title.
Law   340.1   76-17098
ISBN 0-8046-7105-2

Patri meo

"Deus auribus audivimus. . . ."

CONTENTS

PART II — SOCIAL CONTROL: THE MATERIAL CAUSE

PART III — INSTITUTIONS: THE FORMAL CAUSE

PART IV — PEOPLE: THE FINAL CAUSE

PREFACE

"Ce livre est toute ma jeunesse" and a good deal of my middle age into the bargain. One way or another, most of the people I have encountered in twenty years of teaching law have had a part in it. I will mention here only those friends and colleagues from different disciplines who read the manuscript and saved me from all kinds of errors and infelicities: Thomas Shaffer (Law), Stanley Hauerwas (Theology), Peter Walshe (Economics and Government), and Jeanne Rodes (English), who is all the more friend and colleague for being my wife, plus Ernest Szarwark of our Law School Class of 1976, who checked most of the references, and Arabelle Ellsworth, who typed the manuscript.

I have tried to acknowledge my specific intellectual debts as I have gone along. It occurs to me though that I owe a good deal more to Jacques Maritain, Martin Buber, and Jacques Ellul than the passing references I have made to them would indicate. There is also Caryll Houselander, to whom I have not referred at all, though her thought has entered more deeply than I can say into my understanding of the human needs the law must serve. Much of the material in Chapter Eight is based on J. Huizinga's *Homo Ludens*, another work I have not had occasion to mention in text. Other ideas in that chapter I have developed out of a series of conversations with John Julian Ryan, a man who has thought profoundly and beautifully about the Christian doctrine of work and who was generous in sharing his ideas and his hospitality with a young law teacher.

Finally, I feel I have done less than justice to H. L. A. Hart, whom I have mentioned often enough, but always negatively it seems. I am far from wishing to belittle what he has done in renewing the important tradition he represents. Indeed, it is a measure of his achievement that one who disagrees with him as profoundly as I do should yet encounter him at every turn.

I have not tried to document my attribution of doctrines to different authors and schools, except in a few cases where important ideas are to be found (as far as I know) only in law reviews. The main purpose of the reference notes at the end of the book is to cite the cases referred to in text, document the quotations, and give some indication of where I got my legal rules and principles. On the rules and principles, I have not attempted to be exhaustive, but what I have given should enable anyone using standard tools of legal research to pursue the different topics as far as he cares to.

Notre Dame, Indiana

THE LEGAL ENTERPRISE

1

INTRODUCTION

In this book I propose to give a general account of the legal order and how we use it. As the legal order is not really intelligible outside of a concrete manifestation, I will pay particular attention to its Anglo-American form, the one with which I am most familiar. I shall deal with the subject in terms of the four Aristotelian causes: efficient, material, formal, and final. I am not wedded to Aristotelian metaphysics, but I find this particular device useful as a way of putting together the valid insights that different legal scholars have had concerning what they were about. Some have seen law as an emanation of the community or its government — efficient cause. Some have looked at the force behind it, the policeman, the executioner, or other more subtle agencies of social control — material cause. Others have looked at its procedures, its internal logic, and the institutional forms through which it is applied — formal cause. Still others have concerned themselves with its manner of contributing to the welfare of human beings — final cause. To say that a full account must include all four causes should enable us to give a proper place to each of these approaches without excluding the others. The Aristotelian analysis allows me to be, as all good lawyers are, eclectic.

Before I embark on an account based on these four causes, there are three preliminary matters I would like to take up. I suppose I could cover them within the main analytical structure I have projected; indeed, I will probably cover them there, and more than once. They have a broad bearing and for just this reason I would like to consider them at the outset in isolation.

THE SIGNIFICANCE OF THE LEGAL ORDER

The first matter is the meaning of the whole subject, *sub specie eterni-tatis* — what part does law play in the final scheme of things? Speaking as a Christian, I see it as mediating a particularly elemental mode of God's presence in the world of men. Man makes two all but universal claims upon law. One is to vindication against unjust force; the other is to the rudimentary conditions of life. These seem to correspond to God's earliest promises in Genesis: to go on ruling the world, and to let man live. There is no legal system, however flawed or corrupt, that does not have these claims made on it, and, in some way, acknowledge them. So the legal enterprise, by its very existence, seems to mediate God's implementation of these first promises. It is in this way that I take St. Paul's teaching that the pagan rulers of Rome are ministers of God.

It follows that the legal order should be limited in scope. The promises it mediates do not exhaust man's needs or God's response to them. Law cannot deliver man from the predicament in which he finds himself. The best it can do is preserve in man a posture conducive to a deeper encounter with God, or whatever serves him in God's place. Here, it seems to me, is the true ground of personal freedom as we know it in our legal system. Law must leave man free to work out his own salvation because it is not capable of working it out for him.

It does not seem, however, that the limited scope of the legal order can be adequately expressed in such traditional formulations as temporal order or common good. These suggest a materialist conception, as if it were the part of law to be a mere umpire in the struggle for survival, or, if you prefer, a commissary sergeant. It should be seen, instead, as involving the community of mankind, with a common interest in a fully human life for all.

Within a legal enterprise conceived in this way, there can be no absolute authority. I think this is the basis for what we call the rule of law, the principle that no man may rule over another except within prescribed limits. Human authority stands between a God whose ultimate purposes are inscrutable, and a human being whose ultimate being is impenetrable: anyone who makes it a basis for intervening in the affairs of his fellows should do so with humility and reverence. Even at that, law can do only imperfectly what it sets out to do. The best-run legal system will evince a good deal of inefficiency in its work of redressing wrongs and sustaining well-being. If the citizens do not put up with this inefficiency, if they do not accept the rule of law and forbear to take the law into their own hands, the system will break down. We cannot in reason expect this kind of forbearance to be unlimited, but we will never have peace unless there is a good deal of it. For a Christian this measure of forbearance is supported by the fact that no human purpose can fully coincide with the purposes of God. In God, every man is fully vindicated, but often in mysterious ways.

Since this forbearance is necessary but limited, everyone who comes in contact with the law must bear the responsibility for deciding whether or not to exercise it in a given case. To impose or accept the demands of a flawed legal system involves one kind of responsibility, to resist or subvert them another. In either event, the lawyer cannot shift the blame to his client: the citizen cannot plead that he is only obeying the authorities, or the authorities that they are only following the law. Nor can the revolutionary blame the system he seeks to overthrow for the harm he does in trying to overthrow it. Every man is responsible for his own actions. Law is simply another element in the situation within which he must act.

By reason of the mediating role I have described for it, the legal order is distinct from the political, economic, or social order, and from the historical order. It is of course dependent on all of these in many ways, but within its own proper sphere it mediates an authority that transcends them. With this authority, law mediates, first, between the individual and every form of order in the community. If it appears that in a particular case the individual should prevail, then prevail he must despite any political, economic, or social consideration pointing the other way. The principle is embodied in the maxim *fiat justitia, ruat coelum*, let justice be done though the skies fall. This means, for instance, that the fact that a man will endanger the community if left at large does not justify imprisoning him for a crime he did not commit. This is a trivial example: we shall see others more sophisticated as we proceed.

With the same authority, law mediates between the political order and the other orders of the community, economic and social. Through it the political order achieves its economic and social effect, and at the same time the community holds the political order within its proper place. This point I will expand on at some length in Chapter One.

Also law mediates between history on the one hand and both individual and community on the other. It is a vehicle for the community's desire to control its own history: the true meaning, I suspect, of the current agitation for law and order. Conversely, as soon as any historical change has fairly taken hold, the lawyers are at work bringing it home to the community: witness the spate of legislation and constitutional amendments after our Civil War. As for the individual, he looks to law to mitigate or at least predict the effect of history upon him, and to claim those rights he considers immune to historical change: a good deal of litigation in Franklin Roosevelt's days can be understood in these terms.

Finally, law mediates, again authoritatively, between good and evil in the historical order itself. This follows from Maritain's doctrine of the ambivalence of history. Since any given historical situation will contain within it both good and evil, it is always open to human beings by free and intelligent choice to enhance the one and resist the other. Law is a major vehicle for their doing so. Perhaps I can clarify this position by contrasting it with two other doctrines about law and history. The so-called Historical School teaches that law is an emanation of the *Volksgeist,* or spirit of a people as manifested in history and the Marxists believe that law is a projection of the interests of a ruling class. These doctrines agree in making the legal order internal to the historical. In fact, if law were a mere historical phenomenon, they would shed a certain amount of light on it. But speaking as a lawyer looking at history rather than a historian looking at law, I find them not so much false as irrelevant. The *Volksgeist* theory leaves out of account the ambivalence both of history and of the *Volksgeist* itself. Jesse James, for instance, has as deep roots in the American *Volksgeist* as Abraham Lincoln has: I must draw on moral principles outside American history to decide which one to pattern myself on. As for the Marxists, whether their charge is true or false, I know of no lawyer, myself included, who does not consider it a charge, an accusation of wrongdoing. If we serve only the interests of the ruling class, it is because we are corrupt or obtuse or both. We would like to do better.

METHODOLOGICAL ANTINOMIES

When Portia says, "Earthly power doth then show likest God's when mercy seasons justice," she raises a fundamental difference between the legal order and the divine presence it mediates (substitute if you must, here and further along, a philosophical concept of perfect rule). God does not apply justice seasoned with mercy: He is entirely just and entirely merciful at the same time. It is only when His attributes become reflected in human methodologies that they appear in the anti-nomic relation Portia states: to show likest God's, earthly power must sacrifice a bit of justice to blend in a little mercy.

Portia's justice and mercy form only one of a multitude of legal antinomies or oppositions. It seems that lawyers are forever balancing one thing against another, or trying to see which of two things something is when there is good reason for saying it is both. I am suggesting that it is because our methods mediate a divine presence that is not yet realized that these dialectics are continually cropping up. What we experience as opposites are not things essentially oppposed like black and white, but things which our own imperfection or the imperfection of the milieu in which we work makes it impossible for us to deal with except in opposition to one another. All these oppositions are so familiar I need only touch on them here to show what I have in mind. Here are some of the more important ones:

Personal concern versus objectivity.   A human being would probably not consider himself justly dealt with if someone simply fed the raw facts of his case into a computer which printed out a decision. He expects his affairs to be determined by another person to whom he can address himself in terms of their common humanity. At the same time, he will not be satisfied if some official, like the Caliph in the Arabian Nights, disposes of his case in the light of an overall subjective impression, without reference to any principle or standard. He expects an objective standard against which his situation can be measured. No legal order can give him all of what he seeks. The more a legal order achieves objectivity, the more impersonal it becomes; the more personal it is, the more it falls into subjectivity and caprice. What a man really requires is to be judged by God, who is totally objective and totally personal at once. What we try to give him instead is a human being whose personal judgments are limited by objective standards but not overwhelmed by them.

Order versus justice.   God's government of the universe is entirely orderly and entirely just. We, however, continually find ourselves putting up with a certain amount of injustice for the sake of order: our rules of *res judicata* are a fairly noncontroversial example. And, on occasion, we endure a certain amount of disorder for the sake of justice: some of our free speech cases and many of our criminal procedure cases take this form.

Freedom versus righteousness.   Freedom and righteousness are equally attributes of the eschatalogical human being: In Heaven, everyone will do perfectly right in perfect freedom. On earth, though, those who have freedom are apt to exercise it in doing wrong. Lawyers, therefore, are always concerned about how far they should curtail freedom to encourage righteousness, how far put up with wrongdoing for the sake of freedom.

Symbol versus utility.   The divine government of the universe expresses what it accomplishes and accomplishes what it expresses. Human laws, however, are apt to express one thing and accomplish something entirely different. For instance, we have laws against prostitution and homosexuality. Their purpose is to express our commitment as a society to the sexual standards they embody. Their actual result is that prostitutes spread venereal disease, and that homosexuals are blackmailed. On the other hand, the repeal of the laws in question will be taken as expressing society's approval of new departures in sexual permissiveness. A number of controversies, particularly those over unenforceable laws, arise from dilemmas of this kind.

Norm versus fact. In the divine order of things, what is and what ought to be are the same. In this world, they are different, often radically so. The legal enterprise plays an ambiguous role here, sometimes expressing things as they ought to be, other times trying to cope with things as they are. This ambiguity dominates questions like what part empirical data should play in legal judgment, or how far a rule of law should be "administered" by an empirically sophisticated "agency" instead of "interpreted" by the verbal and philosophical wisdom of a court. There is a related question of how far a legal judgment is based on what the law itself is as distinguished from what it should be.

Means versus ends. God is able to accomplish what He wills, and no more than He wills. If we want to accomplish something, we must find a way. Sometimes, no way can be found, or the most effective way does more harm than good. We have to ask questions: How many crimes are we willing to leave unpunished (or, worse, unprevented) in order to avoid tapping telephones? How much pornography are we willing to put up with to protect artistic expression against the evils of censorship? Or, conversely, how much invasion of privacy will we accept in order to prevent or punish crimes? How much artistic expression are we willing to inhibit in order to spare ourselves the indignities of pornography?

Intuitive versus discursive knowledge. God has only one way of knowing. Man can know either by immediate awareness, called intuition, or by inductive and deductive reasoning upon data. Our minds being what they are, the two methods do not always yield the same results. When they conflict, we have made a mistake in one or the other, for truth is unitary; but we have no basis for saying which is the more reliable. A generation ago there were impressive cases where scientific judgments about the economy proved better than crass intuitions about laissez faire. Today, the pendulum may be swinging the other way: intuitive judgments about the environment and the quality of life seem to be proving better than crass administrative expertise. There is no basis for preferring one form of knowledge to the other. The law should offer sufficient scope for considering both.

Choice versus discernment. While some theologians have found occasion to distinguish between God's will and His intellect, it seems as a general matter that what He chooses to establish is identical with what He discerns to be good. Human beings, on the other hand, when they make or apply law, are never sure whether they are exercising a mere choice, or trying to discern something that will determine what they should do. We ask whether judges make or discover law; whether legislators should be governed by the wishes of their constituents, or by their own rationality and expertise; whether the mores of a community arise out of what their ancestors have chosen to do, or out of their understanding of the requirements of human nature. Questions like these affect how we think about law, how we obey it, and how we go about changing it. The emphasis on choice seems to make us more impressed with authority, less with precedent or tradition, than the emphasis on discernment. The wills of our ancestors are buried with them, but their experience lives on. Conversely, I may be wiser or more learned than a judge or a Congressman, but no one has assigned me the work of making choices for the community.

Here too, experience of ambiguity comes from our not being God. Our discernment is continually taking us to the point of finding that something must be done, and leaving us there without showing us just what to do. I discern that my teen-age daughter should not stay out all night, so choose to tell her she has to be in by eleven. As far as I know, ten forty-five or eleven fifteen would have done just as well, but in theory if I had perfect wisdom and knowledge I could pick the optimum time to the minute.

THE GOODS OF THE LEGAL ORDER

Limited both in scope and methodology, law must also be limited in what it can accomplish. It has no complete answer to economic, social, or political questions, and still less a solution to the final destinies of men and nations. A community can have good law and bad politics (say the people have a habit of gratuitously overthrowing the government), bad economics (say they are locked into a one-crop agriculture, or have insufficient technology to employ all their university graduates), or needless to say, bad morals. Law can mitigate these evils, but it cannot take them away. Then, what can law accomplish by itself? What specific goods can a community hope for from good law, independent of whatever else is amiss?

I suppose the first thing is peace. It was said in praise of certain medieval kings that a woman or a child or an unarmed man could carry a bag

of gold from one end of their kingdoms to another without being mo-
lested. For this state of affairs to obtain and to be matter for praise, we
must suppose that the good king not only put down violence but also
stood ready to meet any just claim that anyone might have had to separate
the affluent traveler from his gold. Merely repressive law will insure, at
least for a time, that a man can go about his business in peace; good law
will insure too that he is entitled to peace. If it cannot do away with the
evils of society, it will at least reach anyone who can be identified as personally responsible for them, or anyone who uses his social advantages
so irresponsibly as to give his neighbors a personal grievance.

Good law also supports freedom. It will protect one's openness to
God and neighbor against abuse or arrogance of authority, or interference
by other people. Also, to some extent at least, it will protect his free
development as a human being against stultifying action on his own part
— self-mutilation, destructive drugs, or submission to a too-abject servi-
tude. In many societies, to be sure, the most serious restraints on freedom
arise not from any of these sources, but from the mere circumstances
of the economic or social order. In that case, if law cannot remodel the
society, it would seem it cannot establish freedom. This is true in a way,
but I think not as true as people these days tend to suppose. It seems
to me that circumstantial restraints, however galling, are experienced
differently, and cut less deeply into one's humanity than restraints imposed by the responsible actions (or inactions) of human beings. A person
who is protected against the latter is in an important sense free.

This brings me to the subtlest, and perhaps the most important, of
legal goods. Good law will define your circumstances, hence your existential situation, and ultimately your identity. It will make explicit who
you are, whom you are married to, what your responsibilities are in the
community, and what part of your external environment is subject to
your necessities, your self-expression, your will. Whatever your situation,
law will insure respect for it, and for you in it.

This respect, because it is the root principle of what is due every
man, lies at the heart of the concept of justice, the virtue that moves
us to render every man his due. Justice, in turn, is the essential element
of the contribution good law can make to the general well-being of human
beings. Good law will support justice and render redress whenever well-
being is impaired by the failure of one person to render another his due.
This will not reach every impairment of well-being: many such impair-
ments will be due to economic, social, or political forces the community
has not the skill to discern or the resources to control. But under good
law, the members of the community may set out together to find a way
of coping with these forces.

I

SOCIETY
The Efficient Cause

2

THE DIALOGUE BETWEEN COMMUNITY AND GOVERNMENT PARTICIPANTS

Whenever there is law, there is one human being intervening in the affairs of another. The so-called laws of God, of nature, and the like are important in many ways to the legal enterprise, but they only become so when one person sets out to impose them on another. To the extent that a person accepts them internally, and tries to put them into practice in his own life, it seems better to put them in the realm of morality. To be sure, this distinction between law and morality is not neat. There is a middle ground occupied by cases like the one where you get me to follow your views by persuading me that they are right, or where I adhere to a moral principle that requires me to obey your commands. Some of these matters we will have to take up as we progress, but for the moment it is enough to point out that morality is ultimately worked out in the privacy of one's own conscience, but with law there is always dialogue.

PARTICIPANTS

The legal dialogue does not irresistibly require what we would generally call a community. In theory, some powerful or officious person might impose his views on a number of disparate neighbors who had nothing in common except his intervention in their affairs. This seems to be the upshot of the social contract theory. Proponents of this theory envisage a state of nature in which everyone pursues his own interests, paying no attention to his neighbors except when they get in his way. People emerge from this state by agreeing to hire a functionary called a sovereign, who will make and enforce rules to keep them from unduly interfering with each other. By this act, they become a body politic, and their individual pursuits are subject to the powers of the sovereign. But they have nothing in common except their subjection to him. Needless to say, this account is not meant to be taken seriously as history. Its object is to provide a mythological base for an analytical approach to law: an approach in which the only legally relevant community is the one created and defined by the law itself.

Real life, of course, is quite different. All the law we actually experience is addressed to an ongoing community. It takes its place in a matrix of different human relations, only part of them legal. To my mind, what defines the relevant community is history. This is of course true in the trivial sense that the existence and effect of a law is a matter of historical fact. But more important, the very coherence of the community in which laws operate seems to depend on some common experience or common consciousness of history. I suppose, for instance, the Civil War occupies about the same place in the consciousness of Americans, whether their ancestors were Unionists, Confederates, or Galician peasants. The centrifugal forces in America are provided by people who cannot absorb the prevailing consciousness of Nat Turner's Rebellion, the Alamo, or Little Big Horn. A new enhancement of our national unity will require not a modification of our moral judgment on these events, but a reshaping of their place in our national consciousness. Similarly, it seems that the growth of a common consciousness of the World Wars of this century has had a good deal to do with the developing juridical integration of Western Europe, whereas the emergence of two Germanies seems more a product of two different experiences of the last quarter century than of two different legal, political and economic systems. To take yet another example, it seems unlikely that Ireland will ever be united as long as events like the siege of Londonderry, the Battle of the Boyne or the Easter Rising occupy radically different places in the consciousness of different Irishmen.

The law we are interested in, then, operates on an ongoing community defined by a common history. It operates also on a community with a government. Here again, there is no inexorable requirement. We can hypothesize a community in which every member claims his own rights when he chooses, and vindicates them when he can. The blood-feud and wergild societies of our remote ancestors were in some ways communities of this kind; so is the international community of today. As long as you adhere to some rational basis for defining and enforcing your stake in your neighbor's conduct, we can speak of what you are doing in terms of law. International law, for instance, despite the lack of any real government to give it effect, keeps a good many professional lawyers busy doing professional things. Still, we think of legal forms like this as primitive, imperfect, or otherwise special cases. In the normal course of events, we expect law to be defined, enforced, and at least in part created by some kind of government.

What kind of government is a matter for considerable debate. Of the various answers proposed, the most prevalent, and to me the most attractive, is that nothing is required to constitute a government beyond acceptance by the community. The principle goes back to early conceptions like conquest and seisin, or to the real property doctrine that a possessor has full rights against anyone but the true owner. It took its place in modern legal theory with Austin's definition of the sovereign as the person or body that people are in the habit of obeying. Austin's modern heirs offer a few refinements. Olivecrona, for instance, reminds us that what people do with the mandates of government is something more subtle than habitually obeying them. And H. L. A. Hart points out that the rules that make the government may have a more fundamental place in the public acceptance than the government that makes the rules. But the basic insight is still that the way to find out about the government of a given community is to look and see. In other words, the government, like the community, is a matter of historical fact.

The alternative is to adhere to some criterion of legitimacy. This can be either a formal, as opposed to a historical, acceptance by the community (e.g., by Act of Parliament, or plebiscite), a source outside the community (e.g., monarchy by divine right), or conformity to an a priori ideological principle of what a government should be (e.g., dictatorship of the proletariat). Of these, the one most influential in American life has been the first. Even today, as recent events in Vietnam show, Americans often hold a touching conviction that an appropriate combination of constitutional conventions, ratifications, and free elections can confer instant legitimacy on a government, in the teeth of any historical forces that happen to be pulling some other way. In fact, history is not so easily circumvented, as we are beginning to find out.

As long ago as 1841–42, the point came up with almost textbook elegance in a constitutional crisis in the state of Rhode Island. That state was still governed at the time under its original charter from Charles II; it was the only state that had not adopted a new constitution during or after the Revolution. The charter had an extremely narrow franchise and contained no provision for amendment. The people in power under it were unwilling to support a change. Accordingly, certain citizens, acting entirely on their own, called a convention to draft a new constitution, and held an election at which the resulting document was approved by a majority of the adult male inhabitants of the state. The proponents of the new constitution then declared it in force, and proceeded to hold an election under it, at which one Thomas W. Dorr was elected governor. Dorr then tried to assume the powers of government from the existing authorities, who had consistently ignored these proceedings. There was a brief trial of force, in which Dorr was defeated. He was eventually convicted of treason, and served a brief time in prison. As Austin would have put it, Dorr was unable to break people's habit of obedience to the charter government.

Two sets of judges passed on the legal significance of these events. Chief Justice Taney, speaking for the Supreme Court of the United States, in an elaborately constructed test case (a victim of the charter government's martial law moved to Massachusetts to create federal diversity-of-citizenship jurisdiction), held that the question was a political one which the judiciary could not resolve. In other words, only the government in actual control, the one designated by historical events, could be regarded by the courts. Rhode Island's Chief Justice Durfee, in various criminal proceedings, including Dorr's treason trial, said a few things to the same effect, but took the question of formal legitimacy more seriously than Taney did. He made three points, not altogether consistent with each other. One was that there might be a right of revolution, but it was only a right of successful revolution: if Dorr had succeeded in taking power, the courts he established would no doubt have considered him justified — a reliance on history. One was that the sovereignty of the people must be exercised under the forms of law if the law is to take notice of it — a species of formal legitimacy different from the one Dorr claimed. The last was a kind of social contract argument: a state exists by virtue of its constitution; hence, to dissolve the constitution is to dissolve the state, and vitiate the basis for a new constitution. The upshot of all this was that no one was prepared to give unqualified authority to the naked historical fact of who was in power, but it was that fact that proved ultimately decisive.

Rhode Island got another constitution in 1843, adopted by the same kind of proceedings, but this time with the advance approval and cooperation of the charter government. No one questioned its authority. It appears to be generally held by American courts that a constitution put to the people by a proper vote, accepted by them, and duly put into effect is a proper constitution regardless of whether the previous constitution provided for it. The de facto (i.e., historical) acceptance which Dorr's case showed to be a necessary condition is evidently not a sufficient one. The Supreme Court of Georgia in 1946 was quite prepared to consider whether the constitution put into effect the year before had been lawfully adopted (i.e., whether it was formally legitimate).

In the British tradition, formal legitimacy, represented by Parliament, rather than the electorate, has played a considerable role, evidenced most often by the elaborate parliamentary ratifications undertaken for the various faits accomplis of English history, beginning with the election of William the Conqueror as king by the Witenagemot. But in recent years, three courts in that tradition, the highest courts of Pakistan, Uganda, and Rhodesia, have found a fait accompli sufficient by itself. Each of these courts had occasion to consider at great length the legality of measures taken by a government that had overthrown the constitutional government previously in power. In each case, the court, relying expressly on the doctrines of Hart and Austin, held that the de facto possession of power was sufficient for legal effect.

Ideological and other criteria of legitimacy have played less part in Anglo-American legal history than formal criteria. Prescinding from primarily political movements like the Jacobite, we can point only to a few documents like the Articles of Impeachment against Richard II and the American Declaration of Independence, to a line of cases like the recent one-man-one-vote decisions in the United States Supreme Court, and to a few oddities like Edward IV's attempt to overthrow the Lancastrians by a lawsuit before he did it by force. Anglo-American thought has far more affinity for formality than for ideology. If history prevails over the one, *a multo fortiori*, it prevails over the other.

In many of these cases, the politically minded will fault the judges and lawyers for accepting historical realities that are often politically reprehensible. Would it not have been better, for instance, if the judges in Rhodesia had refused to cooperate with the iniquitous white supremacist regime of Ian Smith? The judges can offer as their spokesman Sir Matthew Hale, who despite his open royalist views, took judicial office under the Commonwealth. He evidently felt that a usurped government needed good judges at least as much as a legitimate one did. This seems fair enough. Note that we are dealing with bad governments, not with bad laws. How good judges should deal with bad laws, we will consider later. The distinction has been insisted on by contemporary German judges, who treat immoral Nazi enactments as nugatory, but refuse to invalidate reasonable enactments simply because the Nazis made them.

THE PLACE OF LAW

Just as there could theoretically be a legal dialogue without community or without government, there could theoretically be a dialogue between community and government without law. We could hypothesize a regime, an extrapolation on the "despotism tempered by assassination" of the Czars, in which a mad dictator ordered people about by mere whim, with no rational basis whatever, until they finally turned on him and replaced him with someone else. Here again, there is nothing quite so bizarre in real life. Any actual government, however outrageous, has rational claims made on it by the community and offers rational justification for what it does. There is always some basis for discerning a legal enterprise.

The different activities and aspirations that make up the legal enterprise all express in one way or another this underlying element of rationality. Constitutional documents, parliamentary law, and political and electoral procedures give a rational form to what the community will accept and what it will demand from its government. Law, decrees, commissions, and precedents structure the government's demands on the community and its members. Through the art of advocacy, the members of the community make and rationalize claims on the government; through that of legal counselling, they are assisted in rationally predicting what the government will do, and acting accordingly. Conversely, through sociological jurisprudence, the government can determine its own actions by predicting how the community will respond.

These different aspects of the legal enterprise correspond in great measure to the accounts of the nature of law offered by the different schools of nineteenth- and twentieth-century commentators. For instance, the Analytical Positivists, Austin, Kelsen, and Hart, regard the formal expressions of government as the proper subject matter of legal study. Austin appeals to these in a simple form: they are the emanations, as we saw, of a sovereign whom people are in the habit of obeying. Kelsen is more complicated. He treats them as norms whose validity depends on their conformity to a basic norm (*Grundnorm*) that is axiomatic for the system under study. In theory, the *Grundnorm* could be anything, but what Kelsen is actually thinking of is a constitution, a norm which defines the apparatus of government and authorizes it to utter more norms. Similarly, for Hart, law is a system of rules that can be recognized by their consonance with a "rule of recognition" accepted in the community. But the rule of recognition he has in mind is one establishing the legislative powers of government. In the British legal system, for instance, he says that the ultimate rule of recognition against which all other purported rules must be measured is that whatever the Queen enacts in Parliament is law. He even says that when a British colony becomes independent it acquires a new legal system by virtue of acquiring a new constitution, a theory I should think the local bar would have trouble accepting.

To my mind, Hart's insistence on a unitary ultimate rule of recognition is the weakest point in the interesting and sophisticated theory he sets forth. Not only does it require us to say that the Statute of Westminster of 1931 produced five new legal systems with two pages of type; it requires us to say that oral contracts would become effective in England tomorrow if some historian were to prove that Charles II did not sign the Statute of Frauds. As far as I can see, the reason Hart places himself in this indefensible position is that he is unwilling to make repeated references to the community to see what rules are in force there. He has to make one such reference in order to establish his ultimate rule of recognition. But if he had to make it too often, he would have to embark on a general empirical study instead of the analytical study he has in mind. He would have to turn his attention from the government to the community not merely at the outset, but repeatedly.

There are schools that devote themselves to observing the community as the source of legal validity. The most influential of these has been the Historical, which sees the task of the jurist as discerning and systematizing the legal phenomena that have developed out of the spirit of a given people, the *Volksgeist*. It is easy to cavil at this approach, as John Chipman Gray does when he asks what difference between the *Volksgeist* of New York and that of Massachusetts accounts for their different rules on certain points of contract law. On the other hand, it is difficult to see what the Supreme Court of the United States has in mind if not a *Volksgeist* when it holds that an American accused of a serious crime cannot have a a fair trial if he is denied a jury, whereas everyone else in the world can.

The Scandinavian Realists also tend to focus on the community, although their methods are semantic and psychological rather than historical. Their concern, based on analytical philosophy, is to get rid of metaphysics. It leads them to suppose that statements of empirical fact are the only form of language that actually means anything: Olivecrona has an interesting demonstration that there is no such thing as a dollar or a pound since we went off the gold standard. Hence, a particular legal utterance, for example the Civil Rights Act of 1964, has no meaning. It is merely a kind of magic formula whose significance lies in the psychological states it induces in those who hear or read it. As an unrepentant metaphysician, I cannot take any of this as seriously as its proponents do; still, it will not hurt to be reminded that the purpose of legal utterances is not to convey information, but to elicit a response.

These English and Continental schools, whether they focus on the community or on the government, seem to take a more academic approach than do the native American schools. Their interest can be characterized as observation and analysis, ours as prediction and control. American authors who focus on the government, therefore, become American Legal Realists. They conceive of their job as one of interpreting the government to the community so members of the community can cope with the government's effect on their lives. The most extreme statement of the position, put forward, perhaps not altogether seriously, by Holmes, would have it that law itself is merely a prediction of what the courts will do in fact, for the benefit of a hypothetical bad man who wants to hold onto his money and stay out of jail.

This approach is more felicitous in the office counselling situation than elsewhere, but even there it has its drawbacks. Even assuming that I am willing to have bad men for my clients, and that predicting and conforming to what the courts will do in fact is a better way for a bad man to stay out of jail than, say, bribing the police, I wonder if I am giving responsible legal advice to my clients when I tell them that they may:

1. Avoid service of process by hiding.
2. Leave the jurisdiction with a child rather than comply with a decree as to his custody.
3. Disregard a contractual undertaking if the sum of money involved is too small to be worth suing for, or if the opposite party is too poor to sue.
4. Engage in any kind of concerted conduct where the participants are too numerous to arrest.

In any of these cases, there may be a moral basis for acting illegally on a given occasion, and a lawyer may quite properly point this out. But it does not seem very helpful to say that this kind of thing is legal merely because the courts will not prevent or punish it.

To be sure, these are peripheral objections. The great bulk of a lawyer's work, at least in the office, rests very comfortably on an understanding of law as a prediction of how the governmental apparatus will respond. When I draft a will, the important legal question is how my testator's property will be distributed. When I draft a contract, the question is how it will be enforced. When I review a title, it is whether my client will lose the property. When I advise on a normal corporate or tax matter, it is whether my client will be sued, and if so, whether he will win. When I advise on settling a personal injury suit, it is how much a jury would award if the case went to trial.

The crucial defect in American Legal Realism is that it stops at the courthouse door. It has no meaning for either an advocate or a judge. The judge trying to decide a case will not be helped by the reflection that the law is anything he says it is, nor will the lawyer serve his client's cause by arguing it in these terms. The American concern with prediction and control, when applied to these aspects of the legal enterprise, produces the Sociological School. For this school, the work of the legal scholar is one of discovering how the law, a means of social control, affects the community in which it is applied, and how it can be modified to produce socially desirable effects. While some of the sociological people, including their leader, Roscoe Pound, took exception to the formulations of the American Legal Realists, they were basically the same people looking at matters from opposite sides of the bench. When you advise a client, you want to know how the government will behave; when you decide a case or enact a law, you want to know how the community will behave. I think most American lawyers would agree.

The approaches of the schools we have dealt with so far can be approximated in the following table.

	OF GOVERNMENT	OF COMMUNITY
OBSERVATION AND ANALYSIS	Analytical Positivists	Historical School Scandinavian Realists
PREDICTION AND CONTROL	American Legal Realists	Sociological School

Of course, these are not all the schools there are, let alone all the ones there might be, but I think they cover a fairly broad spectrum of nineteenth- and twentieth-century thought. Of the doctrines I have left out, the most important ones could be fitted into the classification if we were to prescind from the value criteria that they include in their definitions of law. For instance, Blackstone's reference to "[a] rule of civil conduct prescribed by the supreme power in a state, commanding what is right and prohibiting what is wrong," would place him squarely among the Analytical Positivists if the references to right and wrong were deleted. His "supreme power in a state" has obvious affinities for Austin, while his "rule of civil conduct" is almost what Hart would say. Similarly, the theories that relate law to the common good could probably be assimilated to the Sociological School if the conception of common good could be stripped of its moral implications.

For my own part, I have no intention of excluding moral or other values from an account of the legal enterprise. But I do want to postpone their consideration to a later stage. Our immediate concern is with how law is produced in a given society, and what place it occupies in that society's life. It seems that the legal enterprise as we experience it corresponds in important ways with each of the previously proposed answers, but resists being limited to any one of them. Accordingly, with as much diffidence as is possible in an essentially temerarious undertaking, I would like to offer a synthesis.

I see the essential task of law as one of introducing a rational framework into an ongoing dialogue. People can express their stake in other people's behavior in terms of naked imperatives: "Shut up." "Get out." "Let go." "Give me that." "Leave me alone." "Help." "Off with his head." But we do not have the beginning of law until the discourse is expanded to include a rational basis for what is said: "Shut up, I'm trying to sleep." "Give me that, I had it first." "Leave me alone, I never did you any harm." Without this underlying dialogue, law is unintelligible. Hence, a complete account must look not at one or another of the participants in the dialogue but at the dialogue itself.

Following the example of a number of commentators, notably Hart, I will illustrate with a proposed definition of the legal utterance: "*X* has a right." In a full-fledged legal situation (i.e., one where there is an ongoing community and an effective government), I take this to mean: "*X* has a stake in the conduct of other persons, which, upon colorably rational grounds, the government will expect the community to recognize, and the community will expect the government to enforce." I gloss the terms this way:

Stake in the conduct of other persons — If you have a right to grow crops on Blackacre, that does not mean you are entitled to the necessary rain and sunshine, or to have the crows leave you alone. You are entitled to keep other people from interfering.

Upon colorably rational grounds — It is the colorable rationality that constitutes the legal element: the non-rational conduct of the community belongs to sociology, that of the government to politics. I say colorably rational in order to prescind from the moral evaluation of the right in question. It is often held that nothing can be truly rational unless it is conformable to right reason, i.e., moral.

The government will expect the community to recognize — The term *expect* has elements of both prediction (I expect it to rain tomorrow) and command (I expect my students to read this case before the next class). My object in using it is to fuse the insights of those schools that treat of prediction and those that treat of commands. The fusion is not a piece of mere verbal legerdemain: I think a real synthesis is appropriate. The predicting that interests legal scholars generally has to do with the consequences of making or breaking commands, and the commands that interest them are the ones that show a predictable possibility of being obeyed. Thus, the Analytical Positivists and the Sociological School may both be said to concern themselves with what the government expects of the community: one with analyzing and classifying it and the other with bringing it into line with reality.

The community will expect the government to enforce — Here, the idea of expectation may enable us to fuse the insights of the American Legal Realists on the one hand with those of the Scandinavian Realists and the Historical School on the other. While the American Legal Realists concentrate their attention on the government, they do not suppose that a government can operate in a community that does not in some way accept and encourage it. Consequently, their real concern is what the community actively expects of the government not simply what it passively predicts. The other schools look more directly at the community: they see legal dispositions as lodged in the prevailing psychology, or as emanating from the *Volksgeist*. But they are not oblivious of the distinction betweeen law and social custom. They know that customs about keeping business agreements are legal and those about keeping social engagements are not because the government can be expected to enforce one and not the other. Therefore, they too can be said to concern themselves with what the community expects of the government.

My purpose with this formula, as I said, was to synthesize the different schools by shifting their focus away from both community and government onto the dialogue between the two. The idea of expectation, which is central to the formula, seems appropriate for this approach. If I am having a dialogue with you, I expect you to respond when I address you. I do not order you to, though I would be put out if you did not, nor do I predict that you will, though I would be surprised if you did not. So with the dialogue between community and government. There are occasions when we predict, observe, describe, classify; there are occasions when we command, legislate, give orders, make demands or claims. But what is constant through all this is that each side expects the other to respond.

FORMS OF DISCOURSE

The expectations that government and community have of each other can be articulated in rules. The *protasis* defines a general set of circumstances and the *apodosis* describes what is to be done or omitted when those circumstances obtain. A number of interesting recent works have been devoted to elucidating and refining the place of rules in the legal enterprise, and the manner of using them. However, there is a strong line of thinking, especially in this country, that regards the effect of such rules on actual practice as more or less illusory. There is no basis for total skepticism here; I doubt if anyone seriously supposes that there is. We all know, for instance, that you will have a good chance of enforcing an agreement to convey land if you get it in writing, and a worse chance if you do not, and that the difference is attributable to the Statute of Frauds. Still, it is quite likely that a certain amount must be conceded to the skeptics, and it would be well to determine how much before we proceed.

Jerome Frank discerned two types of skepticism, which he called rule skepticism and fact skepticism. They are not inconsistent, and the judicial process affords some support for both. The rule skeptic points out that to decide that a given set of facts falls within the general categories envisaged by a rule is not a mere exercise in deductive logic. It involves the making of choices, and often choices for which the rule furnishes no sure guide. The fact skeptic adds that even if we had an easy way of fitting facts into a rule, our trial process would offer no adequate basis for determining what the facts were. The rule skeptic does not hold that there are no rules, for Llewellyn, one of their leaders, is very much concerned with getting away from "paper rules" and finding real rules instead. Nor does the fact skeptic hold that there are no ascertainable facts, for their leader, Frank, gives a great deal of thought to finding better and more accurate ways of ascertaining them. And Holmes, the ancestor of all our skeptics, remarks, "General propositions do not decide concrete cases. The decision will depend on a judgment or intuition more subtle than any articulate major premise"; but immediately after this famous dictum he refers us to a general proposition which, "if it is accepted, will carry us far toward the end" of making a decision. What these people are trying to tell us is not that the process of formulating and applying rules is inherently futile, but only that we should not set too much store by it.

By now, some forty years after the major skeptical manifestoes appeared, this point is pretty well universally accepted. Hart, for instance, concedes that rules are "open-textured:" there will be cases of doubtful applicability ("Does 'vehicle' used here include bicycles, airplanes, roller skates?") as well as plain cases ("If anything is a vehicle a motor-car is one"). Gidon Gottlieb has developed a new form of logic, neither inductive nor deductive, which he uses to assemble the appropriate variables, turn them into decisions about material facts, and apply them in drawing inferences from rules. On the whole, I am persuaded by these authors that the skeptics, while they have issued a salutary warning, have not dislodged rules from their central place in the legal enterprise.

There is an additional limitation on the significance of the skeptical approach. It is basically a product of American Legal Realism; hence, it conceives the legal enterprise in terms of predicting how government agencies, mainly courts, will behave. What the rule skeptics are critical of is the efficacy of rules, not as a means of articulating expectations, but as a means of predicting how cases will be decided. What the fact skeptics are doubtful of is not whether you and I know enough facts to determine what we expect or what is expected of us, but whether courts can determine enough facts to fulfill expectations or make us do so. Even if they were right as far as they went, it would still be true that rules are what the government expects the community to live up to, and what the community expects the government to enforce. In the dialogue we are considering, this is how the parties address one another.

To illustrate, there is a statutory rule that a person injured out of and in the course of his employment is entitled to compensation from his employer. If I slip on a pool of oil in the factory where I work, I am probably entitled to compensation under this rule; if I slip on the ice on my front porch, I am probably not. In cases like these there will be very little argument: this is Hart's point. While the interpretation of this rule (i.e., what inferences can and cannot be drawn from it) occupies hundreds of pages in *Larson on Workmen's Compensation,* and keeps great numbers of lawyers, claims investigators, administrative hearing examiners, judges, and even law professors gainfully employed, the disputed cases are few in comparison to the claims that are paid every day without the slightest demur.

However, let us turn to a disputed case. Suppose for instance I have an argument with the man working at the next bench, and he knocks out two of my front teeth. This case may go to litigation. The employer may contend that he pays me to work, not to brawl, and that the fight had nothing to do with the job. The Workmen's Compensation Commission, and later the court, will have to decide whether it is only the innocent victim who is entitled to compensation in case of an assault, or whether it is sufficient if the employment produced a psychological ambiance conducive to fights. Then it will have to decide what we were fighting about, and perhaps who hit whom first. Here is where the skeptics have their day. The rule skeptic points out that the choice of what kind of assaults to compensate for depends not on the meaning of the words "out of and in the course of the employment," but on what you think of the human condition in general and that of the American workingman in particular. The fact skeptic shows that in any event we will never know for sure who struck the first blow, or whether the quarrel was really about my spilling iron filings on my neighbor's bench or about the $50 he won from me in a crap game the week before.

Now let us look at the expectations of the parties. In the first place

I, as the injured workman, expect in this case just what I expected in the case where I slipped on the oil: I expect to be paid. My expectation may have less the sense of prediction and more the sense of demand than it did in the other case, but there is some element of each sense in both cases. In the assault case, I would not bother pressing the claim if I did not foresee some chance of collecting, and in the oil case I would not foresee any chance of collecting unless I made a claim. In each case, the reason I expect to be paid is that I expect my injury to be treated as one arising out of and in the course of my employment. I expect the employer and his insurance carrier to accept it as such an injury, and I expect the Workmen's Compensation Commission to make them do so if they refuse. In the fight case, I expect that my legal arguments will convince the Commission that I am entitled to compensation even if I started the fight, or else that my evidence will convince them that I did not start it. You may be skeptical about the effect of the rule on the decision of the case, but there is no doubt of its effect on the way I present my claim, i.e., the way I articulate what I expect.

The same is true of the employer. In the oil case, he expected from the outset that he would have to compensate me, and that the Commission would make him if he did not. But here in the fight case, he expects not to have to pay, because he expects to win before the Commission. His expectation, like mine, is as much demand as prediction, but he too would not litigate if he did not foresee some chance of winning. He expects the Commission to hold that my injury did not arise out of and in the course of the employment, because he expects to persuade them that there is a further rule that a man leaves the course of his employment when he starts a fight, and he expects his evidence to show that I was the one who started it. He too is articulating his expectations by means of rules.

The Commission, when the case comes before them, will do the same. If they accept my contentions and believe my evidence, they will expect the employer to pay, and will tell him so. They will say that there is no rule denying compensation to one who starts a fight, or else will find as a fact that I did not start it. They will end up holding that my injury arose out of and in the course of my employment: that it was within the rule. If they decide for the employer, they will find his version of the facts, or adopt his version of the rules. They will then expect me to go home and take care of my teeth on my own. Once again, expectations are formulated in terms of rules.

Accept, then, that rules play a major part in the legal enterprise, although they do not yield inevitable results by deductive logic. It remains to be considered just what part they play, and what else, if anything, plays a part with them. The inquiry relates to disputed cases like the one

I just put — not to the great majority of cases, like the one where I slip on the oil, in which no one has any doubt what is expected of him under the applicable rules.

Let us begin by looking at two rules that figure in the fight case. One is that anyone whose injuries arise out of and in the course of his employment is entitled to compensation. This is fully established. The government expects the community to follow it, and the community expects the government to enforce it. It happens to be a statutory rule, but there are judicial rules like the Rule Against Perpetuities that are equally well established. The only question with a rule like this is when to apply it. We have been effectively warned by the skeptics that this is not a mere question of what the words mean. In the doubtful cases, at any rate, there are choices to be made.

One way of making them is to appeal to further rules. To this end, the employer offers a second rule: that a man who starts a fight is not in the course of his employment. This is offered as a rule in our legal system, but is not yet established in that capacity. The employer is trying to get it established. He expects me and others in my position to be subjected to it, and he expects the Commission to give it effect. I expect the opposite, and the Commission has not yet spoken. It is for each side, therefore, to make an argument relating his own expectations to the prevailing expectations of the legal system. Anyone familiar with Workmen's Compensation Law will find this fairly easy to do. It is a well known fact — perhaps it goes with the dialogic character I have been attributing to the legal enterprise — that the arguments in a close case are easier to predict than the decision. Our immediate purpose, though, is not to predict what the arguments will be, but to show what their component parts are. This is harder to do, but a number of writers have made progress on it. The elements they discern, aside from the rules themselves, can be described as principles, analogies, and exercises of, or appeals to discretion.

Among the points I will make in arguing this case are that the Workmen's Compensation Law should be liberally construed in favor of the injured workman, that misconduct on his part is not a basis for denying him recovery and that a situation which develops out of the employment should be treated as part of the employment. Of these arguments, the employer will probably not take issue with any but the third. The others he will meet by pointing out that a deliberate act generally breaks a chain of causation, and that the object of the Workmen's Compensation Law is only to cover risks inherent in the employment. I, for my part, will take issue with the first of these, but not the second.

All these contentions are in the form of what Ronald Dworkin calls "principles." They differ from rules in that they can apply to a case without being determinative of it. If the Commission found that I had started the fight, and that a person who starts a fight cannot recover compensation for the ensuing injuries, the case would be at an end. Or if they found that my injuries arose out of and in the course of my employment, it would be equally at an end for the other side. To hold that a rule is in force, and that the case falls within it, is to decide the case. But an applicable principle may be outweighed in a given case by another applicable principle leading in the opposite direction. Perhaps we can say that a principle is a rule with a *ceteris paribus* clause: it tells what to do in the circumstances envisaged, other things being equal.

Principles embody expectations, just as rules do, and they make their way into the legal system in the same manner. Of the principles I have given as examples, some are fully established: the Workmen's Compensation Commission will expect employers and their insurance carriers to recognize them and the community will expect the Commission to enforce them. Others are merely proposed: like proposed rules, they must be argued for. A proposed rule gives rise to two questions: whether it is indeed a rule of the system, and, if so, whether the facts of the case fall within its terms. A proposed principle gives rise to these plus a third: what weight to give it.

Now let us look at analogies. Assume a reported case in which an employee burned himself trying to give one of his fellow employees a hotfoot. It was held that his injuries did not arise out of and in the course of his employment, because he had abandoned his employment when he embarked on the bizarre and dangerous undertaking that led to his injuries. This is what is known in the trade as a horseplay case. It stands for the proposition (i.e., indicates the existence of a rule) that the initiator of horseplay cannot recover compensation for the resulting injuries. The employer will argue from it that the initiator of a fight should not recover compensation either. This is one form of reasoning by analogy; it goes from rule to rule. You canvass the reported cases, and extract rules from them by inductive reasoning. If you cannot find one that applies directly to the case before you, you find one that presents an attractive analogy, and use it to develop a new rule to cover your case. Lawyers tend to think of this as a logical process, but of course it is not. The categories used in discerning old rules, and the analogies used in developing new ones both depend on choices that have nothing to do with logic. When we say that horseplay cases are one category and personal comfort cases (e.g., going to the men's room, going out for a smoke) are another, it is not logic we are using. Nor is it when we decide that fighting is more like horseplay than like personal comfort.

It is possible to reason by analogy without the intervention of rules. Suppose I find a case of a man who was cracked on the head by a descending dumbwaiter when he looked into a mysterious hole in the wall to see what it was. The court upheld an award of compensation by the Commission: a man does not leave his natural curiosity behind when he goes to work, and he cannot be said to abandon his employment when he indulges that curiosity occasionally. I could make an argument of sorts by deriving from this a rule, or more likely a principle, to the effect that one does not abandon his employment by indulging a human foible, and then contending that the desire to slug my co-worker is a human foible. But I will have trouble establishing either of these points in the abstract. I will do better simply arguing that starting a fight in this particular case is like looking into the dumbwaiter shaft in the earlier one. I will still have the same point to make, that the two are comparable human foibles. But this way I can draw on anything in the factual background of the two cases that will help me make it. I will try to show that the material facts of the two cases are alike. My opponent, meanwhile, will try to show that at lease some of the material facts are different (this is known as *distinguishing* the cases), or that the similar facts are not material.

Again, we are not engaged in a logical process. The entire argument depends on choosing which facts are material. In the case I am using for authority, the only facts that are there are those the court that decided it considered material, and the only ones that the court had to choose from were the ones the parties considered material enough to put in the record. Before I ever see the case, the process has filtered out what the injured workman had for breakfast before he came to work, and what he watched on television the night before. Perhaps it has left in that his job was a dull one. Then I can show that my job was dull too: this may be considered a material similarity because boredom leads people to act foolishly. But the decision whether to consider it so will not depend on logic.

Rules, principles, and analogies are all used in the legal enterprise to express expectations, and concomitantly to narrow choices. At the same time, they cannot be used without making other choices: they reorganize, but do not do away with, the need to choose. The discussion so far has led to the following matters of choice:

1. Whether the facts of a given case fall within the terms of a rule or principle.
2. What weight to give a particular principle.
3. What categories to use in extending a rule by analogy.
4. What facts to regard as material in drawing analogies between cases.

To make these choices, the government exercises, and the community invokes, a quality generally called discretion.

The Analytical Positivists, even Hart, seem to regard this kind of discretion as mere naked will. They are influenced, no doubt, by the ethical theory, "X is good" is synonymous with "I like X", that prevails among Hart's countrymen. Dworkin is willing to impose "certain standards of rationality, fairness, and effectiveness" at least to the extent of criticizing any exercise of discretion that does not measure up to them. For my own part, I would require more than this. I see the exercise of discretion as an art, involving both knowledge and skill.

Let me, following the example of many modern writers, illustrate with the model of a game. In soccer, when the referee sees a foul, he can blow his whistle, stop the game, and award a free kick to the side against whom the foul was committed. But the strategy of the game, and the pleasure the players and spectators get from it, depend on a certain continuity of play. Hence, referees are expected to follow a principle of awarding free kicks sparingly in a normal game. They must use their discretion to see that the game is not gratuitously interrupted, and, at the same time, that foul play is restrained. Also, there are cases in which a free kick would operate in favor of the side that committed the foul by enabling them to reposition their men during the break in play. Accordingly, there is a rule that a free kick will not be given unless it will operate to the advantage of the side it is given to. Here again, the referee must use his discretion: he cannot stop the game to ask the captain of the offended side if he wants the free kick.

Dworkin would say that the decisions the referee must make involve no real discretion, or discretion only in what he calls a weak sense, because the applicable rules or principles purport to tell him what he must decide. There is in theory a "right" decision in each case. It may be difficult to find; reasonable men may disagree as to what it is; there may be no appeal from the referee if he has misapprehended it; but still it is there. I find this line of argument appealing, but in the last analysis I cannot accept it. It does not seem to me that there is only one right way of calling a penalty or deciding a case any more than there is one right way of painting a picture. We know when the referee lets the game get too rowdy or too discontinuous, but we cannot say that any one call produced that result or could have prevented it. As for when a free kick will be advantageous to a side, the question involves the likelihood of a hypothetical future event: If I don't interrupt the game, is it likely that the attacking team will score? Philosophers disagree as to whether it refers to any present reality at all. Although the likelihood of the future event is in a sense a present state of affairs, the variables that enter into the discernment of likelihood are intelligible only with reference to the future event. I cannot see that even total omniscience concerning the present will answer the question beyond debate.

So to state that the referee has discretion in these matters does not simply mean that he is left to his own devices to discover the right answer. On the other hand, it does not mean that he may call or not call the penalties by mere whim. There is such a thing as a bad call, and Dworkin would be putting it mildly if he said that the referee who made one would be open to criticism. Nor are Dworkin's standards of rationality, fairness, and effectiveness sufficient to produce good or at least unexceptionable calls. I am as rational, fair, and effective as the next man, but I would not be an adequate soccer referee because I do not understand the game well enough to exercise discretion properly.

The upshot of all this is that discretion is a matter of dealing knowledgeably with questions raised or left open by the available rules, principles, and analogies. This brings us to a final question: What kind of knowledge is required for the exercise of discretion? For the referee, as we have seen, it is knowledge of the game. For the maker of legal decisions or arguments, I suppose the corresponding knowledge would be knowledge of the life of the community. To say this is pretty much to end as we began. Lifting up the building blocks of the legal enterprise one by one, we find underneath them all just what we might have expected — the ongoing life the enterprise is meant to regulate. Those who participate in this ongoing life have expectations, of one another, of the life itself, in the end, I think, of God. These they expect the government to rationalize, to reflect, to enforce. It is all done in dialogue. The players and spectators at a soccer match expect to exhibit or see a certain type of contest involving certain skills. They expect the referee to see that they get what they came for: if he is in any doubt about it, they will let him know. To this end, he for his part will expect the players to abide by the rules, and follow his decisions, and will expect the spectators to refrain from violence and keep off the field. There are also expectations that people and governments bring to the game of life. But for these we will need another chapter.

3

THE CONTENT OF LAW

The next question is how the ongoing life of a community effloresces into the concrete dispositions — rules, principles, analogies, and exercises of discretion — of that community's legal system. A number of answers have been offered, as well as a number of alternative statements of the question. As with the matters taken up in the last chapter, the various proposals touch in one way or another, but do not at all exhaust the realities of the legal enterprise.

RELIGION, MORALS, PHILOSOPHY, AND THE LIKE

It stands to reason that what kind of a being I think you are, and how I think you should behave will affect what I think should be expected of you, and how I expect the government to treat you. It follows that efforts to pursue the legal enterprise from a standpoint of moral and religious neutrality are foredoomed unless they rest on impossibly narrow definitions of morality and religion. In general, we have laws for the relief of the poor because we think it accords with their dignity as human beings to relieve them. We have laws against race discrimination because we think the races are morally and theologically equal, and people who think otherwise oppose such laws. We forbid a man to marry two wives at once because we think one wife is all he should have. We do not allow a pimp to sue a prostitute for his share of her earnings because we disapprove of his trade, and we disapprove of his trade because we disapprove of hers. These moral and religious judgments are not simply the province of the legislature, or of the judiciary on the discrete occasions when they "make law"; on the contrary, they enter into every phase of the legal enterprise.

This much seems obvious to the point of triviality: only the most doctrinaire of theorists would deny it. The classical and continuing debate over law and morals involves a much narrower question. That is whether a given form of behavior should be prohibited (made a crime) simply because it is immoral, and for no other reason. In an era of considerable change in standards of sex, or at least in standards of talking about sex, the question carries more political freight than most philosophical or theological questions do. Consequently, there is a good deal of hypocrisy in the way it is debated. People who say that the moral judgments on X (= fornication, trial marriage, pot smoking, abortion, dirty books) should not be embodied in the criminal law often intend their argument as an opening wedge for the view that X is not immoral. Conversely, those who raise arguments about the social effects of X (e.g., by contending that the reading of dirty books makes rapists of people) are apt to be really interested in suppressing X simply because it is immoral.

Leaving this disingenuous rhetoric aside, the opposing arguments can be simply put. Against making X a crime one can say that it is in the nature of law to serve social purposes or the common good, and that the enforcement of private morality is not such a purpose. Furthermore, in a pluralist society, one where citizens have different opinions on moral matters, it is inexpedient for the state to identify itself with the views of one faction of its members. Instead, it should try to deal fairly with all views and life-styles. On the other side, one can appeal to a long tradition of enforcing morality. I quoted Blackstone in the last chapter on commanding what is right and forbidding what is wrong. As to social purpose, producing an ambiance conducive to private virtue would seem to qualify. As to pluralism, one can always claim that the pluralist commitment of the society does not extend to the moral matters in issue: we are pluralistic as to religion, but not as to sex, or as to sex but not as to drugs.

For my part, I find the second set of arguments more persuasive than the first. I cannot accept an a priori limitation that would exclude law from something it can effectively and usefully accomplish, and I find no evidence that the things it can accomplish are necessarily all social. Consider, for example, the relatively noncontroversial law requiring motorcyclists to wear helmets. It is possible to contend, and some courts have done it, that such legislation has a social purpose in that it spares the state the expense of supporting the cyclist in a brain-damaged condition, or the county that of removing his body from the highway (though it should be noted in passing that the doctrine that brain-damaged citizens are to be supported, and the doctrine that human remains are to be treated more circumspectly than other forms of highway litter both rest on moral and religious foundations). But this is purely tendentious. The reason we have these laws is to keep improvident motorcyclists from getting themselves killed or injured. And if we can protect a man from the consequences of his improvidence, why not from those of his lust or greed?

The difference of course is that we have no one to characterize the nonwearing of helmets as a matter of conscience, or even as an alternative life-style. Overriding another person's moral judgments on his own life is a serious matter. Still, I cannot see that it is a priori to be excluded. Granted, if we are trying to deal with a person for his own good, we will have to remember that it is good for him to have control of his own affairs. In most cases, this good will probably outweigh the moral good we would choose for him. But not in all cases. If you want to become a drug addict, a slave, a priest of Astarte, or a high-school dropout, I find nothing in the ultimate order of the universe that says the law cannot interfere. This is a complex matter; I have tried to deal with it at length in other works, and will try again later in this one. For the moment, suffice it to say that judgments on both personal and social morality enter into the content of law.

But here, we are considering how the ongoing life of the community gives rise to legal dispositions. As a general matter, moral and religious judgments are formed within your own conscience, dictated by reflection on ultimate realities. It is not apparent how they can emerge from the ongoing life of the community. In fact, it has been suggested that we cannot add a moral dimension to law without acceding to the doctrine of the Analytical Positivists, and having the whole legal system imposed on the community from without.

Here again, we can clarify matters by looking at the dialogue in which law is articulated. My personal notions of what is right or wrong, or of the nature and destiny of man, enter into what I expect, as a citizen, of the government. These notions also determine what, as part of the government, I expect of the community. I use the vague term enter into because, as we have just seen, sometimes I will, more often I will not, expect a person to abide by my views where they differ from his own. But whatever I expect, and however loudly I make it known, my expectations are not those of the community until a good many other people share them, and they will not be those of the government until the community accepts them as such. It is through the mediation of the community that personal expectations develop into law.

We have no lack of examples of how this process works. We have seen, for instance, how school integration was first the expectation of a handful of citizens, then that of the justices of the Supreme Court, and how it gradually penetrated the apparatus of government on the one hand, and the conscience of the community on the other. By now, even the most ardent segregationist would admit that "the law" forbids a school district to maintain one school for black people and another for whites, whereas in 1950 even the most dedicated integrationist would have admitted the opposite. In the interim, though, what you took for "the law" depended in great part on what you believed. We Northern liberals regarded *Brown v. Board of Education* as "law" from the day it came out, whereas most Southern politicians gave it no more credence than Abraham Lincoln gave the *Dred Scott* case. Had we continued our military involvement in Vietnam, we might have undergone a similar process concerning conscientious objection to serving there. There were a wide range of moral judgments on the subject which people were willing to argue for as being in accord with "the law." In matters like this, whatever decisions may be reached in particular cases, clear law is not established until the moral judgment of the community is crystallized. In any event, as long as the legal enterprise is conducted in dialogue, there is no inconsistency in letting personal determinations of moral and religious questions affect community determinations of law.

HISTORY AND CULTURE

The *Volksgeist* was one of a number of concepts that came out of the Nazi era with a bad press. The very word conjures up associations of *Blut und Ehre* or *Morgen die Welt*. The problem is that the spirit of a people, like that of an individual, has both good and bad in it. The pursuit of authenticity undisciplined by moral criteria cannot be anything but baneful in the end, whether for a person or for a state. On the other hand, historical and cultural experience, once stripped of its mystique, has an important part to play in developing the content of a legal system.

Take a fairly straightforward legal question: Can a man be awarded alimony from his wife in a divorce proceeding? There is a constitutional amendment in process that will give a clear answer if it is adopted, but meanwhile, the courts must look to the expectations married people have of each other in our society. There was a time when the answer would have been definitely no. A man was expected to support his wife. He could not free himself from that responsibility even if she was independently wealthy, or earned more money than he did. Alimony represented a substitute for that obligation after divorce, and it was for him to pay. A gradual acceptance in the community of the idea of women working meant that the courts became open to the possibility of not giving a woman alimony if she did not need it. But it was still generally felt that a woman who made money should not be expected to use it supporting her husband, whether during the marriage or after it broke up. However, today, there seems to be a tendency developing to accept marriage patterns in which the main financial contribution is made by the wife. If this gets a firm footing in our culture, it will no doubt be reflected in judicial decisions. The wife will be required to support her husband after divorce as she did before. The matter is one in which the law will track the cultural development in the community, pretty well disregarding past precedent. It would jar a bit to characterize these marital patterns as part of a *Volksgeist*, but in fact they belong to the historical development of a people.

Perhaps a little nearer to the mystical approach is the Puerto Rican case of *Pueblo* v. *Tribunal Superior,* though it is a prosaic question of statutory interpretation that is involved. The statute provided that Spanish and English should be used indiscriminately (*indistintamente*) in judicial proceedings. An English-speaking lawyer, defending a criminal case, read this as entitling him to have the entire trial held in English. No, said the Supreme Court of Puerto Rico, "The medium of expression of our people is Spanish; this is a reality no law can change." The statute can give the English-speaking lawyer or litigant no right except to have the proceedings translated for him as they occur.

It may be possible to meet the human aspirations of women without making them support their husbands, and it may be possible to develop an effective bilingual court system. But appropriate references to history and culture make it unnecessary to try. A people's characteristic aspirations and ways of doing things cannot solve the moral and practical problems of the legal enterprise, but they can provide a focus. This point emerges with especial force from the decision of the United States Supreme Court in *Duncan* v. *Louisiana.* The question was whether the federally-guaranteed right to a fair trial, "due process of law," was violated by denying the accused a jury. The court said it was. Obviously, the moral principle that questions of guilt be fairly determined does not inescapably call for a jury; there are systems as fair as our own in which juries play no part. But, said the Court, these other systems were developing other safeguards while ours was developing the jury. The gratuitous elimination of the jury from an Anglo-American trial is not to be equated with the use of a Continental system of criminal justice by people familiar with it. In short, right or wrong, even if they are not historically or culturally determined, have to be applied in a historical and cultural context.

The judicious perception of context that characterizes a proper historical approach is to be contrasted with the sterile antiquarianism that passes for history in some judicial decisions. The most flagrant example is the *Dred Scott* case, in which the Supreme Court considered exhaustively what people had thought of Negroes in 1787 in order to determine how the Constitution applied to them seventy years later. There are, alas, more recent examples. In 1966, for instance, the highest court of Maryland trotted out all the no-popery rhetoric of the early nineteenth century to assess the meaning of the religion clauses of the Constitution. The theory behind decisions like this is that every legal disposition has a built-in, and perfectly static, intent, which is to be discerned by examining the intellectual furniture the framers of the disposition used: nothing that has happened since their time makes any difference. An understanding of the meaning of history, and its place in the shaping of the *Volksgeist*, can emancipate us from this wooden interpretation of our law. Here is Holmes, stating what seems to me the sound doctrine on the subject, in deciding whether a certain treaty contravenes the Tenth Amendment (powers not expressly delegated to the United States are reserved to the states):

. . . when we are dealing with words that are also a constituent act, like the Constitution of the United States, we must realize that they have called into life a being the development of which could not have been foreseen completely by the most gifted of its begetters. It was enough for them to realize or to hope that they had created an organism; it has taken a century and has cost their successors much sweat and blood to prove that they created a nation. The case before us must be considered in the light of our whole experience and not merely in that of what was said a hundred years ago. The treaty in question does not contravene any prohibitory words to be found in the Constitution. The only question is whether it is forbidden by some invisible radiation from the general terms of the Tenth Amendment. We must consider what this country has become in deciding what that amendment has reserved.

There are a good many cases in which it will behoove us to consider what this country has become.

SOCIOLOGY, POLITICS, AND UTILITY

Law does not always track the historical and cultural development of the community; often, it controls them instead. So one of the most important things law draws from the community is assistance in discerning and meeting the need for different kinds of control. This aspect of the legal enterprise has been much emphasized in modern times, but it is by no means new: you could say it was what Henry II was engaged in when he decided to tear down private castles in order to keep the peace. The pre-ambles of the great medieval statutes have many examples of it.

When you get beyond rudimentary matters like peace, the question to what end controls are to be imposed becomes troublesome. An answer has to be philosophically acceptable, and at the same time yield mean-ingful results in the practical world. Traditional learning offered for this purpose the idea of the *common good*. A good is common if by its nature everyone must enjoy it or no one may. Suppose, for instance, there are six people traveling across a river in a boat. It cannot sink for some of them and arrive safely at its destination for the others. Hence, keeping it afloat and on course is the common good of all those in the boat. Moral-ists in the tradition would add that it is the duty of all of them to take suitable measures to implement that common good. They use a concept called *distributive justice* to call for each one of them to be given his fair share of the work.

It can readily be seen that the typical person will belong to a great number of different groups, each with its own common good. For the dwellers in an apartment house, there will be a common good of keeping the hallways clean or the electrical supply working. For the inhabitants of a neighborhood, it will be a matter of safe streets or trash collection. For larger units, it will be the economy, the money supply, or defense. For the traditional learning, every legal disposition was aimed at some common good, either that of the overall community, or that of some sub-ordinate community in which it applied.

Of course the common good of a community must relate in some way to the good of the people who make it up: the boat is for the passen-gers, not the passengers for the boat. But once we leave the simple boat or apartment house and try to cope with the great affairs of men and states, our notion of the common good becomes increasingly dependent on our particular moral, religious, cultural, or historical views of the good of individuals. Accordingly, some people, who take more seriously than I do the quest for neutral principles, try to avoid the conception of the common good, and find some other purpose for law. Thus, Montesquieu rests legal dispositions on the preservation of the political system, Marx on that of the economic system. Some modern authors have turned to the preservation of the legal system itself as the ultimate goal, which seems much like going back to the medieval goal of keeping the peace. But it is hard to see any of these as solutions to the problem. There seems no good reason for preserving the political or economic order, or even the law itself, unless in the long run they conduce to the good of human beings. In fact proponents of these theories are apt to introduce common good conceptions by the back door. There is no better way of preserving an institution than by running it in a way that most people approve of, and there is probably no better way bf earning people's approval than by doing them good.

Perhaps the real objection to the common good formula (or, better, inadequacy in it — there are occasions when I find it both true and useful) is that it offers no basis for the allocation of limited resources. How much of my time should I spend cleaning the washroom for the common good of the boarders in my boarding house, how much painting a clubhouse for the common good of the members, how much protesting air pollution for that of the whole city? Or how much of my tax money should I spend beautifying the streets in the suburban community where I live, how much educating the future citizens of the whole state? Or where shall we put an airport that has to be put somewhere for the common good of a whole region, but which will ravage the common good of those living in its immediate vicinity? Traditional common good learning tended to solve these problems qualitatively, if at all. That is, it tended to give precedence to the common good of the more important community, without taking quantitative distinctions into account. For instance, I have seen a theological treatise that says that ecclesiastical purposes must take precedence over state purposes, because the church serves a higher end of man than the state. Concede for the moment that the author is right in his hierarchy of institutions; does he really mean that a fire engine on the way to a fire has to stop at an intersection to let a funeral procession go by? Obviously, he does not. He has just not stopped to think about measuring the amount of contribution different common goods make to real human purposes on any one occasion.

The fire engine and funeral procession example is not a serious problem, but other problems in the same form are. Take the question of where to put the airport. The common goods of particular neighborhoods are probably considered in deciding where to put it, but in the typical case, no one will give any thought to the possibility of not putting it anywhere: the possibility that the destruction of one neighborhood outweighs in quantitative human terms the good to the whole region of having another airport at all. And if the common good of the smaller or less important community is not weighed against that of .ne larger or more important, *a fortiori,* individual goods are not weighed against common goods. Theoretically, the proponents of common good learning recognize that the individual has primacy over the community, but they find it very hard to put his primacy in quantitative terms. Thus, if the matter is not one like free speech which is radically excluded from community control, the individual is not apt to get much of a hearing. Do we, for instance, consider how much he loves his house before we decide whether to take it away for a highway?

There is one theory that has endeavored to displace common good learning entirely by a quantitative evaluation of individual goods. This is Utilitarianism, which tries to found law on the greatest good for the greatest number. This too can be a sound approach to many problems. Take, for instance, the question whether a certain community should adopt year-round Daylight Saving Time. Naturally, the people who get up early in the morning are against it, whereas the ones who are out late in the afternoon are for it. There is the question of saving money on electricity if most stores and businesses close for the day before it gets dark. There is the matter of danger to children walking to school in the dark versus that to parents driving home from work in the dark. All these matters of convenience, expense, and safety can be roughly quantified and set against each other. People can agree tolerably well on how much expense they will undergo to avoid how much inconvenience, or how much inconvenience they will put up with to avoid how much danger. So we can weigh all the relevant considerations under this Utilitarian rubric, and come up with an acceptable decision as to what is best for the aggregate of the community.

But there are situations in which the greatest good for the greatest number formulation will yield either a wrong answer or no answer at all. Something has to be added. Say there is a community that suffers from overpopulation. A twenty per cent reduction in population would greatly enhance the quality of life for those remaining. At the same time, living standards are so low that life for the poorest twenty per cent is hardly worthwhile. I cannot see that Utilitarianism offers any ground for not killing (painlessly of course) that poorest twenty per cent. You could say that the wholesale slaughter would brutalize the survivors, and thus be bad for them. But there is no reason why this should be the case if they felt that they were doing the right thing, which, on the Utilitarian hypothesis, they would be entitled to feel.

If that example seems too farfetched, try this one, taken (with a touch of poetic license) from a United States Supreme Court case. One Terminiello, a minor demagogue, is addressing a group of followers in a hall he has hired for the purpose. Outside is a mob, people who disapprove of him and his doctrines. They are throwing bricks, and trying to break down the doors. In the offing, presumably, are tar and feathers, or perhaps a rope. The police, good Utilitarians, arrest Terminiello for disturbing the peace. The mob is more numerous than the audience; hence, the pleasure they take in having him shut up outweighs whatever pleasure the audience might have taken in having him finish his speech. Terminiello's experience of being carted off to jail must be chalked up to the minus side, but it is better than having him tarred and feathered, and better than having a dozen policemen put in the hospital trying to protect him. Whatever edification the community might have had from Terminiello's doctrines, had they been more fully set forth, is outweighed by the disedification of having a riot; besides, no one was listening to him except people already convinced of his views.

Terminiello's conviction, despite its unimpeachable Utilitarian support, was reversed by the Court. To interfere with a man's free speech, the state must have a better reason than the vehemence of the opposition aroused by his views. It is precisely the unpopular view that claims the benefit of constitutional protection: the popular view does not need it. The decision seems sound, as does the decision not to liquidate the poorest fifth of our hypothetical overpopulated community. But to support these decisions, we will have to set limits to Utilitarianism. It happens that if we go back to our common good learning, we will find two principles exactly suited to the purpose. One is that the burdens of the common good go with the benefits. Whatever reasons may justify putting someone out of the community — throwing him overboard, expelling him, exiling him, killing him — you cannot do it simply so that those remaining may have the benefit of a larger share. Another principle is that certain individual goods are not subject to the common good. One of these is the good of communicating with others; this is the foundation of the decision for Terminiello.

Generally, then, it seems that Utilitarianism ought to be subject to the same limitations that have traditionally been discerned for the common good. But we are not done with setting limits to Utilitarianism. Imagine that a local park contains a lake that affords intense pleasure to a handful of Thoreauesque citizens who sit on its shores contemplating the beauties of nature. The Park Commissioner proposes filling it in to make room for baseball diamonds and playgrounds, which will obviously afford pleasure to many more people than the lake does. In Utilitarian terms, the only answer the nature lovers can make is that while they are less numerous than the ball players, their pleasure is qualitatively superior or quantitatively more intense. The qualitative argument requires going beyond the Utilitarian framework. The quantitative one Utilitarianism will accept in theory, but will tend to shrug off in practice because there is no way of making the necessary measurements. Naked Utilitarianism tends to overlook the greatest good aspect of its formulation, and concentrates on the more easily measured greatest number. It favors the crass concerns that most people share over the more refined ones that are different for different people. The only escape is to temper the Utilitarian approach with philosophical judgments about the quality of life.

I think a Utilitarian tradition, modified along the lines I have been suggesting, can be discerned in the concern of modern American legal thought with identifying and balancing interests. An interest is roughly equivalent to what I have been calling an expectation. The idea is that if some people expect one thing and others another we should begin by trying to find exactly what each group has in mind, and how far each can be served without serious harm to the other. It may turn out, for instance, that there is a good place to put a playground without filling in the lake, or that there are adequate opportunities to commune with nature in some other park.

Here is how a court might use the interest balancing approach. A developer builds a shopping center, leasing stores to various businesses, and retaining possession of the sidewalks and parking lots for the customers' use. A labor union has a dispute with one of the store proprietors, and sets up a picket line on the sidewalk outside the store. The developer, pointing out that the sidewalk is his private property, brings appropriate proceedings to end a trespass. The interest of the union is in pursuing its labor dispute in the customary way through peaceful picketing, an interest that would be wholly frustrated if the pickets could not use the sidewalk in front of the store. The developer's interest is a purely theoretical one in controlling the use of his property, or a relatively trivial one in accommodating his tenant. Nothing he is seriously concerned about accomplishing will be affected by the picket line. This formulation of the problem makes it easy for a court to decide in favor of the union.

Naturally, the balancing of interests is not always that simple. For instance, if the union trespassers were trying to organize the developer's employees, the developer would have a far more substantial interest in excluding them. The court would have to resort to considerations outside the data (one or another of those we discussed earlier) to justify valuing the union's interest more highly than the employer's.

A great deal of interest-balancing involves what are called individual versus social interests. An individual interest is your concern with making money, being treated fairly, or being let alone; a social interest is about the same as a common good. Many problems are conceived of in terms of opposition between the two orders: individual interest in burning trash versus social interest in clean air; individual interest in selling a product versus social interest in preventing fraud; individual interest in propagandizing by means of a sound truck versus social interest in quiet streets. Sometimes the common good of a small group is referred to as an individual interest when it is set against that of the wider community: the interest of certain employees in striking for higher wages versus that of the general public in maintaining essential services. Sometimes there will be both individual and social interests on both sides of a question. For instance, when a factory is polluting the air, the social interest in the product or the payroll will have to be laid alongside the individual interest of the factory owner, while the individual interest of a near neighbor of the factory may go with the social interest in clean air.

Thomas Cowan has discerned a kind of interest that is neither individual nor social: he calls it a social security interest. This is the interest of the individual in being provided with something by the community — welfare, Medicare, a house, assistance in finding a job. These are not individual interests because they presuppose community intervention in the individual's affairs; they are not social interests because they are concerned with the separate good of an individual. Needless to say, in recent years more and more of the interests with which the law is concerned have been of this kind.

The identification and clarification of all these different interests has provided a major role for the social sciences in the law. All kinds of economic and social data are relevant in determining what is happening to people under a given state of the law, or what would happen to them if it were changed. The extensive use of such data was inaugurated with the eponymous *Brandeis brief.* It was filed by Brandeis himself a few years before he went on the Supreme Court, to delineate the social interest in regulating hours of labor and working conditions of women. The technique had trouble getting established. There was a case in 1932 in which the issue, under the then prevailing interpretation of the Constitution, was whether ice was a commodity so necessary to the people of Oklahoma that the state could control its manufacture. A majority of the Supreme Court blithely discounted the necessity on the basis of a number of off-the-cuff assertions, including one that people could always buy refrigerators if they could not buy ice. Brandeis, in dissent, laboriously established and documented how badly people needed ice, the economic conditions for its manufacture, and the actual availability of refrigerators in the state.

The Brandeis approach became standard under the New Deal judges, especially the erudite and meticulous Felix Frankfurter. It has become less prominent in recent years (though one or two landmark criminal procedure cases have used it), because the major questions facing the courts have been covered by moral or philosophical positions relatively immune to empirical considerations. By the late 1940s Brandeis-type arguments were unnecessary to sustain economic regulation, and were unavailing to sustain restrictions of free speech. The proponents of race segregation were never able to gain anything with their statistics about crime or illiteracy or what have you among racial minorities. The point is that the use of data is never self-justifying. It depends on some moral, philosophical, cultural, or historical consideration that makes the data relevant.

The progress of the civil rights movement in the courts shows how this works. In 1954, at the moment of transition between separate-but-equal doctrines and integration doctrines, a certain amount of sociological and psychological data was admitted to show that separate school facilities were inherently unequal. Even at that point, Edmond Cahn protested powerfully and persuasively against any reliance on scientific data for this purpose, because he felt that a person of ordinary sensitivity could make this judgment unaided, and that it was dangerous to imply that he could not. Soon afterward, in any event, the courts committed themselves firmly to an a priori principle that the Constitution is color-blind, and there was no further need for data for some time. However, in the past few years new questions have come to the fore: how to overcome cultural deprivation, racial imbalance, or de facto segregation, how to move beyond token integration to genuine equality of opportunity. Here the governing principles are more subtle, and there are empirical questions it might help us to answer: Do black students in fact perform better in racially mixed schools? Do black policemen show more restraint than white in arresting blacks? With questions like these, the Brandeis brief may come once more into its own.

A SYNTHESIS

Let us see how these different kinds of elements — philosophical, historical, social — interact in establishing the content of the law in a given case. Suppose we are considering the legality, mainly under the Fourteenth Amendment, of a plan developed by a local school board to rearrange school boundaries and pupil assignments for racial balance. Supporting the plan are blacks who believe that only schools with white children will be adequately supported by white taxpayers, and that only through integrated education can black children be prepared to take their places in American society. On the same side are whites who see integration as the only way to do justice to their black fellow-citizens, and eventually to achieve a society free from racial tensions. The opposition consists of certain white parents and black militants. The white parents see the plan as inverse discrimination. Even if Johnny, who is white, is not treated differently than his next-door neighbor who is black, white neighborhoods are treated differently from black ones. Besides, for the school board to consider race at all is unconstitutional, because the Constitution is color-blind. The black militants believe the only way blacks can get their children the education they need is to take control of their own schools, which they cannot do if their children are scattered among the white schools.

All these arguments can be restated in terms of the constitutional mandate to afford everyone the equal protection of the laws. The proponents of the plan can say that true equality means integration because segregated education is bad for black children. Appropriate data can be introduced to show that black children learn more in integrated schools than they do in all-black schools. The white parents can argue that equality means that race must be ignored: you must treat a white person the same way you would treat him if he were black, and vice versa. The black militants can say that their own schools are being taken away from them because they are black, and for no other reason. To say that black children cannot get a good education unless they go to school with white children is to say that blacks are inferior. The data adduced in support of the plan are irrelevant, because they presuppose standards of educational performance imposed by the culture and lifestyle of white people. To use such data is a violation of equal protection, because it treats white culture as superior to black culture.

These arguments, whether you accept them or reject them, are all reasonably comprehensible taken in themselves. It is when you try to set one against another that they become elusive. The disputants seem less to be taking issue with each other than to be talking about different things. It is at this point that it becomes useful to identify the different interests being asserted and to see what is the basis of each:

1. The white parents are asserting an individual interest. Their claim is not for any particular kind of education for their children, which would be a social security interest, but for equality of treatment. It presupposes a high-level moral principle: it is wrong for the state to take race into account for any purpose whatever.

2. The black proponents of the plan are asserting a social security interest in integrated education, based on an empirical judgment that the educational needs of their children can best be served in that way.

3. Their white allies are asserting a social interest in an integrated society, based on a moral principle that that is the best kind of society to have.

4. The black militants are asserting a group interest in controlling their own schools. It rests partly on an empirical judgment that this is the best way to meet the educational needs of their children, and partly on a kind of moral judgment that their distinctive culture should be fostered and preserved.

With the interests lined up in this way, we can begin to evaluate them. The first thing to notice is that the white parents are putting their individual interest in not being discriminated against on grounds of race on the same level as interests in free speech, freedom of religion, and fair trials. These are so basic to the root dignity of a human being that competing interests, however pressing, can prevail over them only in extreme circumstances, and in limited ways. If we accept this moral evaluation, the white parents have made their case, and our inquiry is at an end.

But suppose we do not accept that evaluation; suppose we find it possible to condemn the treatment of blacks in our own country and still reserve judgment on the allocation of villages between the Punti and the Hakka in China, the system of personal laws in the Ottoman Empire, or the reservation of certain lands in Hawaii for native Hawaiians. In that case, we will have to look to the exigencies of our own national life for the meaning of equal protection.

Here we can turn to history. The most obvious historical observation is that the Fourteenth Amendment was enacted to protect blacks, not whites. However, we cannot automatically infer that it protects no whites today: that would be a superficial reading of history, like Taney's in *Dred Scott*. But what we can say is that it embodied an aspiration to bring black people into the mainstream of American life. Much contemporary legislation bears this out as does some (alas, too little) later interpretation and application. This reading of history gives powerful support to the social security interest advanced by the black proponents of the plan. Whatever equality requires in other contexts, integration is and has been for a century the chosen path to equality for the American Negro. The white proponents of the plan, for whom integration is a social (as opposed to a social security) interest, can say that the same has been true for all other ethnic groups. Our aspiration has always been to "fashion into one united people the multitudes brought hither out of every kindred and tongue." No minority among us has achieved true equality unless within the framework of the unity envisaged. *E pluribus unum* is central to the American *Volksgeist*.

The black militants have two lines of argument, not altogether consistent. One is that they require some organized control over their own affairs, especially over the education of their children, if they are to prepare themselves adequately to take part in an integrated society. The other is that the goal of integration itself ought to be modified or abandoned in their case as destructive of the human values of cultural autonomy. Each of these arguments has some historical basis — the first in the experience of groups like the Irish that have successfully entered the mainstream, the second in that of groups like the Mexicans that have not.

But basically they are Utilitarian arguments. They propose that a historical process be controlled for the good of the human beings involved in it.

This is where the social scientists come in. With sufficient data, they could probably give a decisive answer to the question of whether black students can master a traditional curriculum better in an integrated school or in a school controlled by their own people and geared to their own needs. In deciding whether integration is served or disserved by the contacts that take place in integrated schools, or whether cultural autonomy is more or less important than integration in giving the black man a just appreciation of his own worth, it is important to listen to the social scientist, though it would be a mistake to give him the last word. When you come to the deeper questions of what a human being is and what his life means to him, human sympathy plays a part that no data can supersede.

This brings us back to history. There is no principle *fiat historia ruat coelum*. Historical considerations cannot override utility, as moral or religious considerations sometimes can. But they can offer a basis for seeing utility in a new light. History offers an approach to whole human beings, including those aspects of them that resist abstraction or quantification. As long as a man does not live by bread alone, it is important in considering what is for his good to know where he has come from, and what he and his society have become. The more ineffable qualities of *Volksgeist* and group identity must be weighed in a subtle balance against the concrete realities of housing, literacy, employment, and the like.

By now it should be obvious that the analysis I have been undertaking will not provide a solution to the question with which I began. What it is supposed to accomplish is to structure the argument along the lines laid down in the last chapter. We have a rule, the equal protection clause of the Fourteenth Amendment. We have a series of contending principles — the color-blindness of the Constitution, the pursuit of integration, the maintenance of cultural autonomy — that will have to be harmonized or else subordinated one to another. All these play their part in a dialogue of expectations. Through the legislatures, the courts, the media, the agencies of both law and politics, each of the parties works to have its own expectation accepted as what the whole community will expect of the government, or the government of the community. But the final decision is a matter of discretion. It invokes the skill of human beings who understand both the legal enterprise and the ongoing life of the community, and can meet the question with a total human response.

II

SOCIAL CONTROL
The Material Cause

4

THE OBLIGATION TO OBEY

OBLIGATION AND SOCIAL CONTROL

In Chapters One and Two we considered how the ongoing life of a community gives rise to the expectations that enter into the law: in Aristotelian terms, how the social order is the efficient cause of the legal order. We must now turn to how people are persuaded to live up to these expectations. Means include the rack and rope of the tyrant, the fatherly admonitions of the preacher or the Internal Revenue Auditor, the bellow of the drill sergeant, the scorn of the teenager, the haughty stare of the society matron, and whatever else keeps us on acceptable paths. The social scientists refer to them collectively as means of social control. I call them the material cause of the legal order because a good lawmaker uses them as a carpenter uses boards or a sculptor clay.

To be sure, some means of social control are more useful to the lawmaker than others. Law is consciously imposed by the government and consciously invoked by the citizen. It would be hard to explain in advance to the matron just when to stare haughtily or to the drill sergeant just when to bellow; hence, these means would be hard to put into a legal form. Of the means actually used by law, the most familiar (so familiar that some authors have considered it the only one) is physical coercion or punishment — payment of money, forfeiture of rights, imprisonment, flogging, or death. Equally serviceable in many cases, more serviceable in some, are exhortation or education, or ceremonial expressions of approval or disapproval — awards and medals, one-day jail sentences, nominal damages, token fines. In other cases, what works best is some modification of the ambiance, the economy, or other extrinsic motivation to conduct — encouraging love of the past by preserving historic buildings, encouraging production by reducing taxes, preventing the extinction of mountain lions by forbidding the sale of their skins. These different kinds of devices for imposing the expectations of community and government have all served their turn in the legal enterprise, and we will discuss them in due course.

The primary means of getting people to live up to expectations is simply drawing on their basic willingness to do so. The lawmaker, by putting an expectation in legal form, creates a legal obligation which affects behavior in the community because most people, most of the time, obey the law. Otherwise, the lawmaker would not be able to function. He cannot use force on more than a fraction of the community, and he will have no force to use unless there are a good many people willing to obey him.

The terminology is tricky here. Law cannot always be attributed to a living and identifiable lawmaker, it often does more sophisticated things than issue commands, and it often requires something more subtle of the citizen than simply to obey. So when we speak of lawmakers making law and other people obeying it (it would be cumbersome and pretentious not to), we must remember that we are using a shorthand notation to describe a more complex process.

The legal obligation the lawmaker imposes must be distinguished from a moral obligation. You have a legal obligation to do something when the government expects you to do it and the community expects the government to make you do it. You have a moral obligation to do something when it is morally right to do it and morally wrong not to. There can be a legal obligation where there is no moral obligation — e.g., my obligation not to put a fence more than four feet high along the street in front of my house. Or a specific legal obligation can be made out of a general moral obligation, as when the United States government turns my moral obligation to contribute to the common burdens of the community into a legal obligation to fill out Form 1040 and pay the amount determined by the table on page 12 of the Instructions. Or a disputed moral obligation (is A obliged to give B possession of Blackacre?) can be made into an undisputed legal obligation (judgment for A).

Though the two kinds of obligation are distinct, they are related: the effectiveness of any legal obligation depends in great part on people's recognition of a moral obligation to obey the law. This recognition is fragile, even in well-ordered communities, and it is often bizarre in the strength or weakness it exhibits in particular cases. But for more than ephemeral success, the lawmaker has to rely on it. People do obey laws from habit or from fear, but both these motivations will eventually fail if they are not supported by a strong core of sentiment that it is generally right to obey laws and wrong to violate them. Without this core, the most passive population will fall into corruption or anarchy, the most cowed into evasion or rebellion. We must, therefore, examine the scope of the moral suasion attached to laws in order to delimit the most fundamental and most effective of the means of social control on which the lawmaker draws.

Obviously, the moral obligation to obey the law is not unlimited. If you are to have any kind of moral life of your own, you cannot give anyone, even the government, a blank check on your conscience. You will have to know what the law requires of you before you can determine what it is your duty to accord. Hence, the duty to obey depends on the content of the law. As St. Thomas Aquinas puts it, a just law is binding in conscience whereas an unjust law is not "except perhaps in order to avoid scandal or disturbance." In other words, if the law is what the law should be, you ought to obey it; if it is not, your obligation is limited to the general one of not making more of a nuisance of yourself than the circumstances warrant.

At this point, if we are not careful, the inquiry will come apart. The question of what laws people ought to obey will take us into moral philosophy or moral theology, while the question of what laws people will *think* they ought to obey will take us into sociology or psychology. To stay in the realm of law, we require a synthesis. Legal study is concerned with rational expectations. The moral suasion of a law, to be rational, must have at least a plausible basis in principle. To rise to the level of an expectation, it must command a modicum of support in the community.

In practice, of course, rational expectations are developed in a rational dialogue. The lawmaker asserts a certain claim on the conscience of the citizen. The citizen weighs it against whatever other claims on his conscience he recognizes, and responds accordingly. The role of the lawyer in this dialogue is to observe it, to rationalize it, and to mediate it, without actually identifying himself with either side. He has neither the expertise nor the mandate of the moral advisor who puts himself in the shoes of another person and says what he should do. But I do not think he is acting responsibly if he simply makes himself a spokesman for the lawmaker by telling people "what the law is" and letting it go at that. It is his business to show as clearly as he can in a concrete case, without usurping the ultimate moral judgment, just what the law claims and where the claim fits in with the life of the community and the life of his client. With this in mind I will take up in the following discussion the governing moral principles, the bases for determining what laws are just. I will deal, somewhat indiscriminately, with what seems right and what seems apt to be accepted, at least in this society. I like to think that the two converge in the long run: that what is in fact right will ultimately be seen to be. However, my immediate purpose is neither to justify the claims of any particular law on the conscience of the citizen nor to predict what the citizen's response will be. Rather, it is to show how the dialogue is structured in this regard, to show what kind of principles the lawmaker will use in commending his law or the citizen in forming his conscience.

This approach in terms of dialogue may give us an easier time with a threshold question that has elicited a number of unsatisfactory answers over the years. If moral suasion depends on the content of a law, if just ones have it and unjust ones do not, what kind of inquiry must you make before you decide whether a given law is a just one? Does the law have the benefit of the doubt or the burden of proof? In the Middle Ages, there were a good many captious people who refused to consider any law just unless they were fully persuaded it was. Their intransigence tended to turn philosophical order into political confusion. To meet this danger, Renaissance and later thinkers tended to create a heavy presumption that laws were just: only on the clearest and most persuasive arguments could you in conscience refuse to obey. This approach has its own dangers. An authoritarian type can make it an excuse for abandoning all personal responsibility for making moral judgments about the law. The prevalence of such an approach among latter-day interpreters of St. Thomas seems responsible for the poor showing of German Catholics in the face of the Nazi regime, and for what some consider the equally poor showing of American Catholics on Vietnam. Contemporary authors, affected by this recent experience, have modified the traditional presumption by carving out special categories — war, massacre, race discrimination — where it does not obtain.

If we recognize that the moral judgment develops out of a dialogue, it will be apparent that whatever presumption may be appropriate pertains neither to the law nor to the individual conscience, but to the dialogue itself. That is, how skeptical the citizen is, or ought to be, of the claim a particular law makes on his conscience will depend on how little confidence he has, or ought to have, in the whole legal enterprise as it is carried on in his society. The question cannot be dealt with in terms of an abstract presumption. Everyone will have his own opinion on it, and the interplay of different opinions will determine the relevant legal situation. In any event, presumptions have no place among the principles in which the dialogue must be articulated. These, as pointed out, are the principles we use for determining what laws are just.

COMMANDS AND PROHIBITIONS

St. Thomas offers three criteria for a just law. It must be enacted by legitimate authority, it must be directed to the common good, and it must distribute fairly the burdens it imposes. There is nothing to quarrel with in the first, but I think the other two need restating. The last chapter demonstrated the inadequacies of common good as a measure of the purpose of law. I would prefer to put the matter more broadly and say that the law must pursue a good end. As to the distribution of burdens, St. Thomas seems to have in mind a matter of having everyone take on his fair share: a tax law would be unjust if it taxed only the poor. But he does not reach the possiblity of a law being unjust because it imposes a burden that no one should have to bear, for instance, an overzealous restriction on free speech. To encompass this possibility, I would eliminate the reference to distribution, and say simply that a just law must pursue its end by fair means. Let us say, then, that a just law is one that is enacted by legitimate authority, that is directed at a good end, and that pursues its end by fair means.

The requirement of legitimate authority (competence, constitutionality, *intra vires*) insofar as it can be divorced from the others, gives only a modicum of trouble. There are those (the I.R.A. is an example, I suppose) who adhere to some criterion of political legitimacy, and deny that any enactment of a government that fails to meet that criterion can be binding in conscience, however innocuous its content. But as we saw in an earlier chapter, most people are willing to accept that a de facto government is legitimate until it is replaced. Within a given governmental system, there are subordinate authorities of limited competence, but the scope of their powers is generally tested by higher authorities in the same system, rather than by the individual's conscience. For instance, it would be a cantankerous individual who continued to feel that a regulation of the Federal Trade Commission exceeded the statutory powers of the Commission after the Supreme Court had held it did not.

Competence as such, then, raises serious moral questions only in cases that fall on the boundaries between one legal system and another. Questions of territorial limits are the most usual. If I am a citizen of Erehwon living in Ruritania, am I morally bound to pay the Erehwon income tax? If I am a Ruritanian fisherman, am I morally bound to respect

Erehwon's unilateral extension of her territorial waters two hundred miles offshore? Those who take seriously the claims of an institutional church may find other examples. For instance, a man may feel he is morally bound to attend Mass when the ecclesiastical authorities say to, but not to vote the way they tell him to. Conversely, certain canonists feel that the marriage laws of the state are not binding in conscience because marriage is the exclusive province of the church.

Questions like these are interesting, but peripheral. The serious problems are raised by laws that emanate from legitimate authority, but seem unjust because they do not pursue a good end, or because they pursue it by unfair means. In this category are laws that go beyond the legitimate concerns of the community by requiring immoral behavior or infringing on personal rights, laws that contribute to an unjust or oppressive ordering of society, and laws that fail to pursue a good end because they are ill-advised, misinformed, or merely frivolous. Each of these presents special problems.

The easiest to deal with is the law that requires immoral behavior: i.e., calls upon me to do a specific act that I consider intrinsically evil — killing innocent people, participating in a form of worship in which I do not believe, returning an escaped slave to his master, leaving my brother's corpse unburied. It is clear that in conscience I must disobey. If the act is intrinsically immoral, the law cannot make it otherwise, and I have to do what is moral rather than what is legal. Furthermore, I think I may resist if I choose the imposition of the punishment I incur for disobedience. Here, I am in opposition to a venerable doctrine supported by Socrates, by the High Anglicans of the seventeenth century, and in modern times by Gandhi. All of these teach in one way or another that, while my conscience may require me to disobey the law, it does not require me to stay out of jail; rather, I owe it to peace and good order to go to jail when the community wants me there. To my mind, this doctrine takes the community too seriously. The witness of Socrates and his hemlock was profound and admirable, but hardly compulsory. The community has no particular right to be edified in this way at the expense of one's life or liberty. A human being has rights that the community did not bestow, and cannot abrogate, whether for edification or for public order. Among these, surely, is the right not to be punished when one has done nothing wrong.

Similar to laws that put people undeservedly in jail are laws that impair basic or traditional freedoms such as the freedom to marry the person of your choice, or to speak your mind on the issues of the day. In a particular economic and social context, you might find equally objectionable a law that interfered with your freedom to change your residence or your job. These are not like laws that require immoral acts; you can comply with them without doing anything wrong. But it does not seem that you have a moral obligation to do so. It is legitimate for the community to restrict rights of this kind: your right to marry by requiring prescribed formalities, your right of free speech by not letting you use a sound truck at midnight, even your right to stay out of jail by making you answer accusations and if necessary stand trial. But it has no business taking these rights away or making it impossible to use them meaningfully. A law that makes it impossible for lovers to marry, for authors to publish, for innocent people to stay out of jail, can have no moral force. Of course there are couples for whom it would be immoral to marry, books it would be immoral to publish, and perhaps even people (e.g., typhoid carriers) for whom it would be immoral to run loose. But, it does not seem that the law can add to their number.

In our society, we have less difficulty with laws that impose specific immoral acts or abrogate specific individual rights than with laws that contribute, often in subtle ways, to an unjust ordering of society. Everyone will have his favorite candidates for this list, and this is not the place to settle controversies over how our society may be more justly ordered. But let us say a person decides that a certain percentage of the tax revenues of the United States government is being spent on the prosecution of an unjust war: Does he have a moral right not to pay that percent of his taxes? Or if he thinks it unjust that a landlord should continue to collect rent without making repairs to the premises, may he withhold the rent despite the law that says he must pay? May a schoolteacher violate an injunction against a strike when he believes the strike is necessary to get his colleagues fair wages, or his community competently staffed schools?

Let us look at the schoolteacher more closely. Suppose his motivations are entirely altruistic: he will retire this summer, and the wage rates which the strike is about will not go into effect till the following fall. So the injunction does not interfere with any personal right or even personal interest of the teacher's. And of course it does not require him to do anything immoral: it requires him to teach school. His objection to it is simply that it produces a bad result in the community. In St. Thomas' terminology, it is not for the common good.

Accordingly, what the would-be striker should do when deciding whether he is morally bound to obey is to weigh up the social effects on both sides: see whether, as Thomas puts it, obedience is necessary "to avoid scandal or disturbance." How much, then, will the strike disturb the peace and good order of the community? How much will the example of striking teachers break down respect for law in other aspects of life? How badly will children's education be interrupted? On the other hand, how much likelihood is there of the strike accomplishing what it is meant to, and how important will that accomplishment be? In short, to the extent that the general good of the community is your justification for breaking the law, you must satisfy yourself that that good will in fact be served.

The disobedience the school teacher contemplates can be called *civil* disobedience. The term is broadly used these days, but I would reserve it for disobedience motivated by social utility or the common good, rather than by considerations of personal morality or personal rights. People who disobey the law for such purposes are acting politically: they intend to modify the civil order, the order of the state, rather than disregard it. This is why, in deciding what their moral responsibilities are, they ought to consider what is best for the community, rather than how far their own duties to the community go.

Note that on my analysis the justification of any particular act of civil disobedience is a matter of balance. It involves weighing in every case the quantum of disruption against the quantum of good to be achieved. Here I seem to be at issue with most proponents of civil disobedience, who lay down rigorous conditions for embarking on a course of civil disobedience at all. They end up allowing it only in cases of great moral urgency, and only after all normal channels for changing the law have been exhausted. In practice, they have approved it as an expression of opposition to colonial rule, to race discrimination, and to the Vietnam war. I am not sure how they feel about the Welsh nationalists who chop down English-language road signs in Wales. They seem to disapprove of the householder who parks his car across his favorite cobblestone street to keep the city from paving it over with asphalt.

I see no justification for this kind of earnestness about the law. Despite its profound relation to divine providence and human need, law is an everyday affair. It aims for humanity, decency, and order in small matters as well as great. If it operates to the detriment of these values, it can be disregarded unless the disregard will be more detrimental than the law. It follows that small acts of civil disobedience to protest small wrongs are as justified as great acts to protest great wrongs. A man who prevents petty bureaucrats from imposing a cloying uniformity on the streets of his neighborhood may not be as important or as noble as one who mobilizes public opinion against an oppressive police force or an unjust war. But neither is negligible.

In many cases, civil disobedience involves violating laws that are not unjust, and do not contribute to an unjust state of affairs. Suppose an opponent of the Vietnam war, after refusing to report for induction in the Army (personal morality), advising others to do the same (exercising personal right of free speech), and burning the records of his local draft board (civil disobedience directed against unjust law), decides to chop down the flag in front of the local court house and burn it in the middle of a busy intersection during the rush hour. Laws that forbid the destruction of expensive and innocuous public property, and laws that forbid obstructing traffic are in no way unjust; it is quite likely that the laws forbidding disrespect to the flag are not unjust either. Is it permissible, then, to violate these just laws with a view to protesting, and ultimately improving, an unjust situation more or less extraneous to them?

I think my answer would have to be a cautious yes. I invoke caution because the line between civil disobedience and sour grapes is difficult to draw in the heat of controversy, and a good many people cross over it. If you have a serious purpose, if your conduct is open to no moral objection except that it is against the law (it is one thing to chop down the flag, and quite another to cosh the custodian who tries to stop you), if the injustice you are trying to overcome substantially outweighs the disruption you bring about, and if there is a fair chance that what you have in mind will actually contribute to mitigating that injustice, it is probably all right to do it. If, on the other hand, your object is *épater les bourgeois,* to annoy fellow citizens whom you despair of bringing to your way of thinking, or generally to express pique at the intractibility of the whole situation, you are probably doing wrong. In short, civil disobedience is political action, and should be carried on no less responsibly than other forms of political action. It should be carried on also with no less tenderness for the right to disagree: it is as wrong of you to disrupt a rally in favor of the status quo as it is of the police to break up your rally in favor of something else.

To illustrate some of the problems raised by civil disobedience, let me refer to a case on which I am particularly ambivalent. In 1970, a South African rugby team visited Britain for a series of matches with local teams. A number of people decided to protest South Africa's racial policies by disrupting these matches. To this end, they harassed the South African players between matches, made commotions in the stands, attempted to stop play by swarming on the field (generally the police stopped this), and in one or two cases (though many protesters thought this was going too far) scattered tacks on the field. There was some debate as to whether all this was a sound political tactic. A few people suggested that friendly contacts with more liberal societies would encourage the South Africans to liberalize their own country. But the militants argued that the white South Africans were a sports-minded people, and that exclusion from international sport would be the best possible way to bring home to them the odium in which their system was held by the rest of the world. On this level, the militants seem to have the better case. A harder argument to meet is that people who play and watch rugby matches are exercising a personal right to the pursuit of happiness, and are entitled to be let alone unless they are acting immorally or hurting other people. Political agitation can claim no more control over individual rights than political authority can, and political authority would be no more justified in keeping segregationists from playing rugby than in keeping polygamists from drinking sasparilla. To be sure, this argument is not conclusive. The demonstrators might reply that the South Africans are playing rugby not as individuals who enjoy the game, but as representatives of their country, or of groups within their country that share responsibility for its institutions (e.g., segregated sports clubs). This is as far as I have been able to take the argument, and I am not sure what my final judgment would be if I had to make one. However, the point I want to bring out is that since civil disobedience is a political act, it is subject to any relevant limits on political abridgment of personal rights.

PERMISSIVE LAWS

So far, we have been talking about laws that can be thought of as commanding or forbidding something, and we have been asking whether there is a moral obligation to obey them. But some laws can better be regarded as permitting or authorizing something. Then the question is whether we may in good conscience take advantage of them. In some cases, the relevant considerations are about the same as those we have already discussed. If an act is immoral, you cannot do it when the law permits it any more than when the law commands it. If a right is one which the community should not invade, a law permitting private persons to invade it is no better than one invading it directly. This much is fairly smooth going. The problems come in two types of cases. One is where a law serves a legitimate community interest by impinging on a legitimate private interest. The other is where a law is unjust in its overall effect, but you do not harm anyone in particular by doing what it permits.

The main question in the first category is the purpose of the law. For instance, when a statute of limitations provides that I need not pay a debt that has not been pressed for a certain number of years, its object is to protect people against having to refute trumped-up claims that date from so far back that the evidence may have been lost. This is a legitimate purpose for the law, but it should not morally justify me in refusing to pay a debt I know is not trumped up. On the other hand, where a debt is discharged in bankruptcy, there is a strong argument for saying that the moral obligation is discharged with the legal. The object of the law is to give the debtor a new start. It would not be much of a new start if all his debts were still a burden on his conscience. At least until he is back on his feet, he should feel no moral obligation to pay them.

In other cases of the same category, the moral judgment may depend on a context that is affected by the law. Here is an example. People generally recognize a moral obligation to support their indigent parents. Accordingly, Old Age Assistance laws provide that you must reimburse the state for assistance furnished a parent whom you could have afforded to support. Generally, though, these provisions are a dead letter, because enforcing them is more trouble than it is worth. But repealing them seems to bring on a drastic increase in applications for assistance, presumably because children no longer feel that they ought to support their parents rather than let them apply for assistance. We may suppose that the idea is not that the legislature has repealed the commandment requiring support for indigent parents, but that the Old Age Assistance law has become a resource of the parents that keeps them from being indigent. The moral obligation is the same, but the occasions for fulfilling it have changed.

Some cases in this category lend themselves to a formal analysis which may provide some insight, although it cannot be pushed too far. The point is well stated by the Doctor in St. Germain's *Doctor and Student.* The Student has asked whether a twenty-year-old who "hath reason and wisdom to govern himself" may in conscience take advantage of his nonage to recover a piece of land he has conveyed. The Student, relying on the purpose of the law protecting minors, argues that he may not:

Me seemeth that, forasmuch as the law of England in this article is grounded upon a presumption, that is to say, that infants commonly afore they be of the age of twenty-one years be not able to govern themselves, that yet, forasmuch as the presumption faileth in this infant, that he may not in this case with conscience ask the land again. . . .

But the Doctor argues this way:

And upon what law should that conscience be grounded that thou speakest of? for it cannot be grounded by the law of the realm, as thou hast said thyself. And methinketh that it cannot be grounded upon the law of God, nor upon the law of reason: for feoffments nor contracts be not grounded upon neither of these laws, but upon the law of man.

The Doctor will make the minor pay back the money he received for the land: he does not say why, but I suppose he uses the general principle that you must give back money you have been given under an expectation you do not propose to fulfill. But he will not let the purchaser keep the land because there is no principle of law or morality that entitles him to do so.

This line of argument can be applied in various contexts. The law cannot authorize me to steal your property, but it can affect what property is yours. It cannot free me from the moral obligation to pay my debts, but it can have a good deal to say about what is a debt of mine. Thus, in some cases of bankruptcy, I might argue that my undertaking was not to pay for my new refrigerator at all events, but to pay for it unless I went bankrupt. An excuse like this would not look very good in the case of the fifty dollars I borrowed from a friend, but in an installment purchase transaction, surrounded by legal formalities, there might be some merit in saying that the basic undertaking was to do no more than the law required

On my other category of permissive laws, I think I can give a more definite answer. Where a law permits you to do something that is neither immoral nor harmful to anyone in particular, I can see no reason why you should not take advantage of it, even though the law may contribute to an unjust ordering of society. For instance, if you are standing in front of a rest room which the law reserves to members of your race, it seems to me that you should feel free to use it, rather than sacrifice your health, comfort, or dignity to the principle of racial equality. You are not harming any member of the excluded race by using the facility, and you would do him no good by not using it. What you owe him is to support a change in the law. In the same way, it would seem that if the tax laws unfairly discriminate in your favor (say you are an oil producer who considers the depletion allowance unfair), you are still entitled to pay no more tax than the law requires. Here, you have two obligations in justice. One (social justice) is to support a more equitable tax law. The other (distributive justice) is to bear your fair share of the common burdens of the community. The first of these obviously does not call for paying a tax until the law has been changed to require it. No more does the second. Unless the authorities in the community determine how much and in what manner you must contribute to the common burdens, these questions are for you to decide. If you feel that the taxes you pay are less than your fair share, you may be morally bound to contribute further, but not necessarily in the form of a higher tax.

UNWISE OR FRIVOLOUS LAWS

To be unjust in the sense of not directed to a good end, a law need not be as perverse in its enactment or as pernicious in its effects as most of those we have been considering. It may well be that the legal dialogue will cast up a legal disposition which the government and most of the community fully believe to be the best way to meet a particular need, but which you or I regard as a hideous mistake. In our judgment, such a disposition would be for a good end in its intended, but not in its probable, result. May we, then, disobey it on the ground that it is an unjust law?

The school districting plan dealt with in the last chapter shows how a question like this might come up. The proposed plan might be adopted after a full and careful debate that showed its proponents to be men of great intelligence and good will, sincerely committed to giving black children the best possible education, while you or I might still be persuaded by the black militants that blacks cannot get an adequate education for their children except by controlling their own schools. In that case, we would have to say that the plan was in a sense not for a good end, and therefore unjust.

It seems to me that we must nevertheless give it a fair chance to achieve its intended result. Note that this view goes farther than the obligation alluded to in the case of the striking schoolteacher, which is not to disrupt the community more than the cause is worth. It may well be that we consider the deleterious effects of this plan more serious than the measures we might take (e.g., letting air out of the tires of schoolbuses) to oppose its implementation. What I am suggesting in the present case is that we should defer to authority and treat the law as a just one, at least until the deleterious effects we anticipate have become generally apparent.

Our disagreement with the authorities is not a matter of conscience — the discernment of right from wrong — but of prudence — the discernment of the best means to a given end. The philosophical concept of prudence is related to the legal concept of discretion which we considered in an earlier chapter. We might say that discretion is prudence applied to the rendering of judgments according to law. Since it is right to act prudently and wrong to act otherwise, prudence is generally regarded as a moral virtue. But we exercise it by investigating and formulating the answers to questions that are not moral. Questions like how to educate people, how to preserve the environment, or how to check inflation are not moral questions, and the moral urgency of educating people, preserving the environment, or checking inflation will not make them so. If you disagree with someone on questions like this, it does not mean that you have different perceptions of right and wrong. You cannot properly call your disagreement a matter of conscience.

It follows that you are not violating your conscience if you accept the claims of authority in a case of this kind. Once this is recognized, those claims of authority become very persuasive. Someone has to make a decision for the whole community. Since there is no moral question in issue, you have no more moral basis for expecting other people to adopt your decision than they have for expecting you to adopt theirs. Unless the decision can be referred to authority, it will be impossible for the community to move on the matter at all. Giving practical direction to the community in meeting its needs is what authority is for.

Of course, the case is different where the decision concerns your own affairs rather than those of the community. Suppose, for instance, due to some kind of mistaken identity, you are convicted, after an entirely fair trial, of a crime you did not commit. I should think you would be morally justified in escaping if possible, instead of going to prison. As always, you must weigh competing duties to the community and to other people: you probably should not blow up the courthouse, and you certainly should not shoot the policeman who is trying in good faith to execute the sentence, but you have no moral duty to accept the sentence, as you would if you had actually committed the crime. The case is like the one just discussed in that there is no moral question, no matter of conscience in issue, but it differs in that your freedom, unlike the educational system, is not at the general disposal of the community. It cannot be justly taken away when you have in fact not committed a crime.

Another kind of unjust law that presents special problems is the one that fails to meet the criterion of a good end not because it is evil but because it is frivolous. Suppose there were a law forbidding beards. Suppose further that you wear a beard not for any deep personal fulfillment or ideological commitment but simply because you feel like it. Ought you, in deference to the law, to shave it off? Note that the law does not ask anything immoral of you. Nor, as I have put the case, does it interfere with any right of yours that is not at the disposal of the community. Indeed, from the standpoint of the lawmaker, who presumably has an esthetic preference for clean chins, it may be said to have a good end.

The objection to it is that if the wearing of a beard is a mere whim on your part, the suppression of it is equally a mere whim on the lawmaker's. Other people do not have a sufficient stake in whether you wear a beard or not to afford a moral basis for a law on the subject. For this reason, I would consider the law unjust and not binding on you in conscience.

What if the people who enacted the law were motivated by an urgent conviction that it was highly immoral to wear a beard? Or if this seems too farfetched, consider the case of Prohibition, where a vital moral concern of the lawmaker leads him to interfere with the simple pleasures of his fellow citizens. Can he make it a moral duty for me to forego my glass of beer? I have already shown why I think it is a legitimate concern of the lawmaker to encourage what he supposes to be virtue and to suppress what he supposes to be vice. Against this concern of his, I have no very high ground to stand on. I drink beer for the same reason another man wears a beard: I like it. But where the law has no purpose other than the enforcement of a principle of personal morality with which I disagree, I think this is a sufficient reason for not feeling morally bound to obey. Since the judgment behind the law is moral, not prudential, I do not believe I am bound to defer to authority on it. I would hold that while the legal implementation of a principle of personal morality is legitimate, the resulting law can rise no higher in conscience than the moral principle on which it is based.

JUST LAWS

Traditional moralists, in addition to teaching that you are not bound in conscience to obey an unjust law, have discerned two cases where you are not bound to obey a just law either. One is a *merely penal law*, where the authority who enacted it will be just as happy to exact the penalty for violation as to have his law obeyed. The other is where no one else obeys the law, so that obedience on your part would subject you to more than your fair share of the common burdens of the community. An example would be if income tax evasion were so common that no one paid more than one-third of what the law required. Both these lines of argument present difficulties.

The idea of a merely penal law rests on the view that the power to bind the conscience and the power to exact a penalty are parallel means of social control available to the legislator, who can, if he chooses, make use of the one and not the other. I cannot accept this, because it seems to me that the power to bind the conscience is an inherent quality of the law, not just another means for its enforcement. We have seen that a just law is one adopted for a good purpose: it exists because someone in authority has decided that good will come of doing what he commands or evil of doing what he forbids. The obligation to obey his law, then, is simply the obligation to support the good or avert the evil he has in mind. There can be no question of the penalty being an acceptable alternative.

There are cases, to be sure, where the legislator would just as soon exact the penalty as have his law complied with, but these seem all to involve unjust laws. A speed trap is a good example. The town fathers of Arcadia Corners impose a 25-mile-an-hour speed limit on the portion of U.S. 215 that passes through their jurisdiction on the way from one metropolis to another. With the resulting fines, they pay the policeman and the justice of the peace that enforce the speed limit, and they build a new gymnasium for their high school. There is no doubt this is a merely penal law. Its intentions would be wholly frustrated if everyone complied with it: the school basketball team would have no place to play, and the policeman and justice of the peace would starve.

But to the extent that its purpose is to collect fines rather than to slow down traffic, it is an unjust law. It places the financial burdens of the community that enacted it on passing motorists rather than on the members of the community. Hence, it does not distribute fairly the burdens it imposes. I think this is generally the case with laws that are merely penal in the intention of the lawmakers. The relation between the end served by complying with the law and the end served by submitting to the penalty is so tenuous that the overall effect of the law must be capricious, and the law itself unjust.

The reason the merely penal law continues to have a place among moral philosophers who admit that just laws are binding in conscience seems to be the doctrine of probabilism, whereby you may in good conscience follow the views of any respectable batch of teachers on a particular question if it suits your purpose to do so. There are respectable teachers who admit the existence of merely penal laws, and, on this theory, you can follow them on this point in your personal affairs even though your overall system of moral philosophy is entirely inconsistent with theirs. In states that forbid gambling, many a parish bingo game rests on this foundation. It is a weak one. There are respectable teachers if you like who admit the theoretical possibility of a purely penal law, but there are none who establish that, say, the constitution and laws of the state of Indiana concerning gambling are among them. In fact, there are voters and legislators in Indiana who think that these laws should be enforced to the hilt and gambling entirely put down; there are others who think they should be repealed or let pass into oblivion; and still others who think they should be enforced against professional gamblers while church bingo and turkey raffles should be let alone. But there is no one who thinks that gambling is perfectly all right for the community as long as fines are regularly collected and jail sentences regularly imposed.

The law that other people violate seems to present a stronger case than the merely penal law. It would be a harsh rule that said I was morally bound to keep my store closed on Sunday though all my competitors were open, or to insist on having my house assessed at full value when all the other property in town was assessed at one-third. On the other hand, I am reluctant to accept an argument which says that if corruption or evasion becomes general, decent people should feel free to participate in it. I think it would be better to cope with the problem by a more sophisticated understanding of what law is, instead of a more cynical approach to the necessity of complying with it. I previously talked about law as something the government expects the community to comply with, and something the community expects the government to enforce. If that is what the law is, then there is no law where I live (regardless of what you read in the statute books) requiring businesses to close on Sunday, or requiring real estate to be assessed at full value. In short, where people generally do not obey a law, we need not obey it either, not because it presents an exception to the principle that we should obey just laws, but because it lacks one of the qualities of a law.

The advantage of this approach as I see it is that it permits a responsible attitude toward the dynamics of the law. As long as rule is completely dormant on the books, it probably does not matter what ground you adopt for not obeying it. But if it begins to show signs of life —say a reforming administration is working for a more equitable enforcement of tax laws—you owe it to the community to do your part in the development of new expectations under it. You cannot do this under a doctrine that permits you to take no notice of it at all until other people start obeying it.

The traditional excuses, then, for disobeying a just law seem less than persuasive. But the view that there can be no excuse is not very persuasive either. Most people (myself included) do not feel they are acting immorally when they park overtime at a meter, roll through a stop sign in second gear, or walk on the grass in the park. Nor do they feel that the laws they are violating on these occasions are unjust. Unless everyone is suffering from a peculiar moral obtuseness on this point, there must be some kind of moral basis for occasionally disobeying just laws. I find such a basis in the observation I made earlier on that the moral obligation is not an extraneous attachment to a law, but an inherent aspect of it, identical with the obligation to support the good and evert the evil the lawmaker has in mind. From this I derive what I call the principle of selective compliance, which is that the moral obligation to comply with a law is selective: it extends not to everything covered by the law, but only to what is required for the law to achieve its purpose. On this basis, it is probably all right to park overtime if there is plenty of room for other people, to go through a stop sign if you slow down enough to be sure nothing is coming on the cross street, to walk on the grass in a sufficiently unfrequented spot.

These examples, of course, involve laws with fairly straightforward purposes. In other cases, a person may well have a good deal more trouble discerning the purpose of the law well enough to measure the scope of his moral obligation. But I am not proposing that everyone become a student of legislative history in order to understand his duties as a citizen, any more than I would propose that he become a sociologist in order to understand his duties as a neighbor. To take an adequate moral stance in society often requires a sophisticated knowledge of what is going on. This one acquires not through specialized research, but through reflective participation in the life of the community. Law is neither an exception nor a special case. A person who understands his moral responsibilities because he understands his life will also understand how the law fits in.

Note that the principle I have been enunciating is a moral, not legal principle. Whatever it does for your conscience, it will not stand up in court if you get a ticket. But there is a related, though not identical, doctrine which the old theorists called *epikeia,* which justifies you legally as well as morally if you depart from the letter of the law in a case of necessity: if you go on the grass to rescue a child from a dog, your defense will stand up in court as well as in conscience. The idea is not that you have an excuse for violating the law, but that actually you have not violated it, because under the circumstances it is not meant to apply.

Both the moral principle of selective compliance and the legal principle of *epikeia* relate to the discretion I referred to earlier, whereby the soccer referee does not call penalties if they will disrupt the game or be disadvantageous to the offended side. All these concepts and doctrines have in common their recognition that law is neither a game nor a set of magical rites, but a rational ordering of ongoing life, to be used intelligently for that purpose.

CONCLUSION

Put together, the views I have been expounding may give the impression of being anarchic. Many people who address themselves to problems of this kind feel that law and order will be at an end if everyone feels free habitually to measure the law against his own moral criteria before deciding whether to obey it or not. Even granting that conscience must ultimately be followed, they would have you prefer it over law only where the clash between the two is both stark and inescapable. Law, they seem to insist, is something serious: disobey it if you must, but at least agonize over the decision before you do.

From this standpoint, I think the real objection to my approach is less that it is anarchic than that it is not neat. While it would have people obeying the law most of the time, you could never be quite sure in advance when they would and when they would not. It is an objection I cannot so much answer as discount. The legal enterprise is not a self-consistent structure laid over society at selected points: it is a dialogue with all of society's ongoing life. Whatever its internal aspirations to rationality, it cannot but be subject to all the uncertainties and confusions of that life. Where the legal system interacts with the tendency of human beings to distinguish right from wrong and act accordingly—not just on state occasions, but all the time — the situations will be fuzzy at the edges. No law will command the adherence of free people except through some kind of moral judgment on their part. I have tried to give a systematic account here of the grounds on which such moral judgments rest, but certainly I have left a good deal for the individual to decide. If the result is not to be anarchic, it will be because the society is one in which people habitually make room for each other, and treat responsibly their institutional arrangements for doing so. If a society lacks this kind of mutual respect and responsibility, I do not think we can develop an adequate substitute for it by cultivating a servile attitude toward the rules of law.

Just laws embody just expectations. Their primary efficacy for social control lies in the willingness of most people most of the time to live up to what is expected of them. This much the lawmaker can rely on. If he understands what he is about, he will need nothing more. He is not making laws in a vacuum, based on a detached observation of utility or common good. The making of a law is a step in a dialogue: a variety of expectations have gone into it, and a variety of other expectations are created by it. To order all these expectations requires discretion on the part of everyone involved — the legislator deciding what he will call for, the policeman or judge deciding what he will enforce, the citizen deciding what he will obey. This discretion, as we have seen, grows out of a knowledge of the life of the community: knowledge not of an observer, but of a participant.

5

EXTERNAL CONTROLS

Needless to say, the moral obligation of a particular law, important as it is, will not be universally felt, and will not be invariably lived up to, even by those who feel it. Accordingly, we expect the government to *enforce* a law, that is, to support it with some means of social control over and above its inherent moral suasion. To choose appropriate means for the purpose is part of the work of making laws. This chapter will cover the means there are to choose from, and how they can be used. The means include a wide range from the gently supportive or educative to the harshly coercive or punitive. With all the variety that is possible, it is idle to try to draw hard and fast lines betweeen one kind of device and another. The classification I have adopted here is merely for convenience in bringing the whole range under scrutiny.

ORIENTATION

Ever since the 1950s when American courts and legislatures began working actively for the enhancement of civil rights, we have been hearing about the "educative" function of law. The notion was developed to justify the intervention of law in a situation where it ran afoul of strong social convention, and where little could be hoped for from direct enforcement, i.e., coercion. If we are familiar with the recent history of civil rights, we can see what the proponents of this educative function had in mind. Still, our customary understanding of education would have to be stretched a good deal to cover all the things law was supposed to accomplish, and in considerable measure did accomplish, in the field of civil rights.

Only one part of the effort was truly educational. That was the patient work of administrative staffs from some of the pioneer Civil Rights Commissions in persuading employers that their businesses would not fall apart if they hired a few blacks. Here the law played a part in opening people's minds, because threats were in the offing: the administrator could issue orders if he failed to persuade. The threats would not have been powerful enough by themselves to make employers stop discriminating, but they were enough to make them listen to other reasons for doing so. This kind of negotiation from strength is characteristic of the administrative process in areas as diverse as securities regulation and air pollution. To the extent that it elicits compliance by showing the citizen how he may reconcile his own purposes with those of the law, it can be said to achieve an effect through education. The approach has come in for criticism lately, because its emphasis on cooperation tends to make administrators overly sympathetic to the people they are supposed to regulate, and thus to stand in the way of sterner measures. But there is no better way of attacking well-entrenched practices with limited resources.

Another thing the civil rights laws and decisions did — something I suppose you could call educational, though that seems a rather bloodless way of describing it — was draw attention to the moral issues involved, evoke a growing *prise de conscience* in the community. People who had never thought about the matter began to see race discrimination as an injustice. People who had always seen it as an injustice began to see it as an intolerable one rather than one of those you put up with for fear of something worse. The difference between this effect and the one taken up in the last chapter is important, although a little difficult to state. The sense of a moral obligation to obey would lead a person who had thought, and continued to think, that race discrimination was morally licit to abandon the practice because the law said to and it was right to obey the law. The *prise de conscience* would lead him to change his mind on the moral question, and decide that race discrimination was morally wrong. There were certainly a few segregationists who felt the moral obligation to obey and gave up segregation merely because the law said to, but the *prise de conscience* bit more deeply into the national life, and was a far profounder effect of the law.

This particular effect of law does not usually appear in isolation, but there is one interesting example of a case where it does. That is the restraint placed on the Canadian Parliament by the Canadian Bill of Rights. This is an Act of the Canadian Parliament, enumerating certain rights that the people of Canada have enjoyed in the past and ought to enjoy in the future. Since it is not a constitutional provision, it cannot tie the hands of the Parliament, and it does not purport to. All it says is that no act of the Parliament of Canada inconsistent with any of the enumerated rights shall be given effect unless it expressly states that it shall take effect notwithstanding the Bill of Rights. All it does to future legislators is make them publicly face up to what they are doing. In all probability, that will be enough. Provisions requiring administrative agencies to hold hearings, or employers to state the reasons for firing their workmen, aim at the same thing. So probably do the health warnings on cigarette packages; they can hardly be conveying any new information. Similarly, many fair housing laws allow a seller to discriminate but forbid his real estate broker to do so: if the seller wants to discriminate, he must confront the would-be buyer and turn him down personally; he cannot use the broker as a shield for his conscience.

To my mind, the most important accomplishment of law in the field of civil rights has been the imparting of a new élan to the opponents and the victims of race discrimination. There is a tendency (not inescapable, witness Prohibition) for what is illegal to be considered not socially respectable. Hence, the urge to conformity, present in most people, powerful in many, can be enlisted in the service of a given social policy by a careful use of laws and decisions. The law achieves its effect partly by creating social pressure in support of the favored policy, more by giving a basis for resisting social pressures the other way. Thus *Brown* v. *Board of Education*, and the various Civil Rights laws of the 1950s and 1960s encouraged black people to claim their rights more aggressively, and whites who supported them to do so more vigorously. They produced a climate of debate in which segregationists were defensive and their opponents lofty, instead of the other way around. They gave a person who sold his house to a black man something more persuasive than his own moralizing to offer his irate neighbors. They did not by any means provide every qualified black person with a good education, a house, or a job, but they contributed to mitigating the situation.

This élan effect is exhibited inversely in our laws relating to sex and obscenity. A few years ago, it began to be suggested, plausibly enough, that policing the sexual behavior or the reading habits of consenting adults was no concern of the law. In the forefront of the argument were people, such as Anglican bishops, who professed to believe in traditional moral standards, but opposed punishing those who thought or acted otherwise. Accordingly, legislatures, especially the British Parliament, began repealing old laws against fornication, adultery, or sodomy ("the detestable abominable crime against nature" as some statutes put it) while courts began extending wider constitutional and statutory protection to topless dancers and dirty books.

The effect of these changes in the law has not been merely that people now do with impunity what they formerly did in some fear of the law. There has been what commentators on the social scene are calling a "sexual revolution." Whether there is more sex going on now than before is a moot point, but sex is certainly going on in a different spirit. The change in the law has led the sexually liberated to insist, often loudly, that they have a right to do as they do: chastity and even heterosexuality are matters like the observance of Yom Kippur or attendance at Mass; it is bad form to impose your standards on others, or to discriminate against those who disagree with you. No doubt the change of laws would not have been sufficient by itself to bring this new set of attitudes to the fore, but it certainly helped.

Here again, the law cannot be understood as a self-contained body of rules. It is a dialogue with the whole life of the community. The making of a new law or the repeal of an old one elicits not a single response but a whole texture of responses. These in turn have further effects on the law, and thereby produce further effects on the community. If you provide for issuing contraceptives to teen-age girls in order to escape the social consequences of illegitimate births, girls who have previously been deterred from sex by fear of pregnancy will take it up, and moralists will begin saying that the availability of contraceptives requires a basic re-examination of our attitudes toward sex among teen-age girls. If you provide for legal abortions this week because women are dying from un-sanitary and incompetent illegal ones, next week you may find travel agents growing rich bringing pregnant women into the state. The week after you may find a woman suing her doctor for malpractice because he refuses to abort her, and the week after that you may find doctors rou-tinely performing abortions for fear of malpractice suits. If you legalize prostitution because it is so hard to enforce the laws against it, you may find a man complaining to the Civil Rights Commission when he is put out of a brothel on account of his race. One day you may find prostitutes claiming Occupational Disease Law benefits for syphilis, or a secretary being refused unemployment compensation because there is plenty of work available as a prostitute. Effects like these may or may not be desir-able, but anyone who proposes a change in the law without anticipating them is either naïve or hypocritical.

These different effects—education, *prise de conscience,* and élan—seem to me all to arise from a basic role of law in orienting the society. We have already noted that the law is in some measure a product of the *Volksgeist*; it should not surprise us to find that the *Volksgeist* is in some measure a product of the law. A society's laws, like its ceremonies, celebrations, and other corporate manifestations, give symbolic content to its aspirations and its sense of identity. Accordingly, changes in the law both reflect and influence the progress of debate over what kind of society it is to be. There are many laws on the books whose proponents see in them not so much a chance to lean on the opposition as a symbolic vindication of their own claim to constitute the mainstream of society. Being in the mainstream is an advantage that many people (the Amish for instance) can be quite comfortable without; even so, most of us will think twice before we decide to forego it. When the law takes a stand, even if it is not effectively enforced in any obvious sense, it tends to impart a certain historical direction to society. This tendency is a basic means of social control, and one often overlooked by those who advocate "law reform" in simplistic utilitarian terms.

Social orientation is brought about not only by more or less unenforceable laws directly specifying desired conduct, but also by enforceable laws on peripheral matters. For instance, if an employer is determined not to hire black people, he can probably get around the antidiscrimination laws. But he cannot get around a law that forbids him to advertise for whites only, or one that forbids him to demand photographs with job applications. Enactments like this serve the basic policy against discrimination in two ways. Obviously, they make discrimination a little less convenient. More important, they make it a good deal less conspicuous. The employer may still be getting away with discrimination, but the fact that he is doing so is no longer so apparent in the community that other violators are encouraged by his example, or victims discouraged from trying to enforce the law.

In short, if you cannot suppress an undesirable practice, there is much to be said for driving it underground. In doing so, you contribute to a social ambiance free from offensive manifestations of the practice, and render a measure of community support to those who wish to eschew it. Even more than with civil rights, this approach dominates our treatment of the so-called victimless crimes: drugs, gambling, and, at least until recently, sex. Some laws on these matters apply only to more or less overt behavior: public intoxication, streetwalking, meretricious cohabitation, disorderly houses, bucket shops. Others apply across the board, but are enforced only where behavior obtrudes on the attention of the authorities by its blatancy or scale. In most states, for instance, a group of friends playing penny-ante poker violate the same law as does the proprietor of a million-dollar floating crap game, but we would be surprised and probably indignant to see them prosecuted with him. Similar distinctions are made with sex offenses between consenting adults, if they are prosecuted at all, and are coming to be made with marijuana.

This kind of enforcement goes back to the discipline of the medieval church, which had a set of judicial procedures for correcting notorious sinners denounced as such by their neighbors, whereas secret sinners were left to the confessional. The idea was that *scandal* made the sin the business of the community instead of the private problem of the sinner. Indeed, a person who led his neighbors to think he was doing something wrong might be put to penance for the scandal even if he was innocent.

The main objection to protecting the ambiance by selective enforcement of general laws is that it places heavy reliance on the discretion of policemen and prosecutors. There is nothing spelled out in the law that prevents them from breaking up friendly poker games, lying in wait for high school students who pick wild marijuana, or interrogating motel patrons to see if they are married to each other. For this reason, there is some tendency to say that laws that cannot be systematically enforced without infringing unduly on private lives should not be enforced at all. Thus, the Supreme Court of the United States held that a law against using contraceptives was unconstitutional because it invaded the privacy of the bedroom. To me, this seems a strawman. In our present social context, there is no likelihood on earth of police, with or without warrants, invading people's bedrooms to catch them using contraceptives. In fact, the law was used against people who actively and publicly advised and assisted its violation. If it was unconstitutional, it was because people should be allowed to use contraceptives, not because their privacy needed protection.

In all probability, we ought to regard the Supreme Court's treatment of contraception as *sui generis*. If the Court were to adopt a general principle that any law that would be intolerable if enforced to the hilt cannot be enforced at all, we would have few laws left. The need for discretion, as I tried to show earlier, is not a peculiarity of certain laws; it cuts across the whole legal system. British trade unionists have long known that working to rule, i.e., following rules to the letter without using discretion, is as damaging to their employers as a strike. So the Chicago police recently were able to give dramatic expression to a grievance by ticketing every traffic offender they could find. The authorities will make a botch of enforcing any law unless they know what the law is supposed to accomplish, and act accordingly. If a law has the orientation of society for its primary purpose, we should see that it is enforced with that purpose in mind. In fact, we generally do.

INDIRECT MOTIVATION

Legislating on peripheral matters can also affect motivation in more specific ways than by orienting the society. As an example, Llewellyn refers to a city ordinance that virtually eliminated pilferage of books from the library by forbidding book dealers to sell any book with a library stamp. With no ready market, no one was motivated to steal books from the library except for his personal use, which made the volume of theft pretty well negligible.

Indirect motivations of this kind are limited only by the ingenuity of the lawmaker. Among the examples that occur to me are putting bumps in roads to keep cars from speeding, encouraging thrift by forbidding employers to pay wages in taverns, protecting alligators by forbidding the sale of alligator-skin bags or shoes, preventing murder by requiring an insurable interest to take out a policy on someone's life. Use of devices like this is a recognition of the dialogic quality of the legal enterprise: a recognition that imposing a policy on a community entails some awareness of what the community is willing to have imposed. If you look at the Theodosian Code, product of a decadent Roman society, ruled over by emperors bemused with the doctrine that their will was law, you will notice a great lack of such devices, along with manifestations of a growing anarchy. Instead of seeing what people could be persuaded to do through the available means of social control, the emperors continued to issue direct orders, backed with increasingly severe penalties. For instance, when the burdens on municipal officials in the provinces became so severe that they began running away from their jobs, the emperors could think of nothing better to do about the situation than to order out troops to capture them and return them to duty. A less authoritarian and more sophisticated government would have found ways to make the job easier.

One form of indirect motivation that requires special consideration is that established through the tax laws. Arranging taxes to encourage particular economic and social patterns is a common device in modern states. Much of the work of mitigating the hereditary class system in England has been accomplished through heavy death duties. In our own country, industrialization was encouraged in the last century by protective tariffs, and in this century technological improvement has been encouraged through special depreciation allowances on income taxes. The balance between public and private social services depends in great measure on the tax deductions available to people who contribute to private charities. If we chose to, we could develop tax incentives for diminishing air and water pollution, or for employing great numbers of unskilled laborers. A judicious modification of the tax laws can accomplish almost anything in the way of economic or social effects.

Tax theorists tend to object. They see an ideal tax law as one that meets and fairly distributes the common burdens of the community, and is at the same time economically and socially neutral. They see any attempt to implement economic or social policies as an intrusion upon the chaste elegance of what they are trying to achieve. But in a broader perspective, taxation as a means of social control has formidable advantages. Since it draws heavily on the self-interest of the citizen, it achieves its effects with a minimum of administrative effort, hardly more than would be required in any event to collect the revenues. Because it brings about social changes indirectly, it creates less feeling of general upheaval than would otherwise accompany changes of the same order. Finally, and to my mind most important, tax laws do not deprive people of the power to make their own decisions about their own affairs. They are impersonal factors to be taken into account rather than orders to be obeyed. They are a change in the cards you hold in the game of life, rather than a stranger looking over your shoulder and telling you how to play. In the modern state with its heavy demands on the public treasury, taxation will necessarily bulk large in the life of the citizen. Its use to effectuate extraneous policies through indirect motivation will probably increase both in scope and in sophistication.

There are problems in relating indirect motivation to other forms of social control. In the first place, its intense pragmatism can work against subtler forms of motivation through social orientation. This tension, for instance, underlies the controversy over whether the government should supply drugs to addicts. The pros are in terms of indirect motivation. The government could drive pushers out of business by undercutting their prices. As pushers are often responsible for recruiting new addicts, putting them out of business would reduce the incidence of addiction. Since a staggering amount of crime is committed by addicts raising money to meet the high cost of their habits, providing them with drugs at nominal cost would greatly reduce the crime rate. The cons appeal to social orientation. For the government to make drugs freely available (and any restriction on availability would sharply reduce the effectiveness of the proposal) would encourage people to use them. The argument is difficult to resolve, because as far as one can see both sides are right. The proposal raises a genuine dilemma, one fairly typical of those with which lawmakers are confronted.

Another problem is the one that arises when laws directly implementing a social policy raise indirect motivations that operate in undesirable ways. Our welfare programs are studded with examples and supposed examples. We are constantly being told that the availability of welfare encourages people not to go to work, or that the cutting off of benefits if they earn any money has that effect, or that women have illegitimate babies in order to get higher payments, or that husbands desert their families because payments are available only to children deprived of a breadwinner. Which of these charges you will believe depends on your politics, but certainly some of them are true. By the same token, there is evidence that minimum wage laws tend to increase technological unemployment by encouraging businessmen to automate, and that workmen's compensation benefits for epileptic seizures make it impossible for epileptics to get jobs. The point is that indirect motivations are constantly being evoked by the law, whether for good or ill, so that the lawmaker must take them into account even when he is legislating with something else in mind.

FORCE

There are many things the law or its minister can make people do or be. Some of these are inherently legal: whether a man can make, or has made, a will or a contract, whether he is the owner of Blackacre, the President of X Corporation, the Sheriff of Cook County or the husband of Susie Jones are all questions the law can answer definitively for whatever the answers are worth. Beyond this, through the intervention of suitable officials, it can deliver actual possession of land and goods, custody of children, and the like, or turn enough of your property into cash to satisfy people entitled to compensation at your hands. Then there are things the authorities can get you to do by inflicting or threatening to inflict pain of some kind if you do not. Criminologists may argue over whether the prospect of going to prison makes many people refrain from murder or mugging: a question we will look at shortly. Social workers may point to its shortcomings as a way of making husbands pay alimony. But no one has yet complained about its effectiveness in getting employers to bargain collectively with their employees when ordered to do so. Similarly, the prospect of paying high money damages does not do much to keep drunk drivers off the road, but it does a good deal to make store and restaurant owners concerned with the safety of their patrons.

The use of these different kinds of force to control particular situations, to prevent particular anticipated harm, or to put right as far as possible harm that has already been done is called *relief*, or the affording of *remedies*. Force applied to someone on account of something he has done, for a purpose other than this kind of relief, is called *punishment*. The threat of a punishment, when made to particular people or in a particular situation, may be a form of relief. When made to the general public, it is part of the *criminal law*. What we accomplish with the criminal law, and what our justification is for inflicting punishment, is one of the classical problems of legal theory; we will take it up shortly. But let us look first at the use of force for relief.

The different forms may be classified as follows:

1. *Modification of legal status or legal rights* — Current examples are naturalization, suspension or revocation of licenses, foreclosure, discharge in bankruptcy, adoption, instructions to a trustee, appointment of an administrator, declaratory judgments. From other legal systems or other times, we can add excommunication, outlawry, civil death, manumission, and filiation.

2. *Exercise of physical control over persons or property* — Transfer of custody of children, commitment of mental incompetents, lepers, or typhoid carriers, repossession of automobiles or furniture, transfer of possession of land, execution of judgments by selling off the assets of the debtor, padlocking premises where illegal activities are going on, razing substandard buildings, destroying infected animals, etc.

3. *Money judgments* — This category, the workhorse of private litigation, at least in our system, is in a way a combination of the first two categories. When handed down, a judgment that *A* pay so many dollars to *B* is a debt like any other (category 1), except that if *A* does not pay, *B* can bring ancillary proceedings to have his property sold (category 2) to raise the money.

4. *Orders backed by threats* — The usual form this category takes in our system is the *injunction*, an order spelling out what a person is to do or refrain from doing. Violation of an injunction is a contempt of court, for which the violator can be put in jail. There are a number of variants, such as the cease and desist order of an administrative agency, which the court will turn into an injunction if it is not obeyed. Another form is the requirement of a bond by which a person undertakes to forfeit a specified sum of money if he does not, for instance, faithfully carry out his duties as a trustee, executor or contractor, or if he fails to keep the peace.

5. *Coercion* — In this category are unpleasant consequences visited upon a person not after he has done wrong, but until he does right. This is often the second stage in the enforcement of an injunction: if you fail to comply, you can be put in jail until you do comply. Other examples are liens and distresses (i.e., chattels belonging to a debtor which you may keep until the debt is paid), and in the old days, imprisonment for debt.

The first purpose for which the law draws on this armory of devices is the enforcement of legal rights and obligations. "Pay what thou owest" and "Restore to me what is mine" are among the earliest of the claims which legal systems have recognized. In our system, the first leads usually to a money judgment, the second to a transfer of possession by the sheriff, though there are sometimes other forms of relief where these will not work. Nowadays, we have added to the list more sophisticated obligations: "Support your family." "Take care of employees injured on the job." "Send your children to school." "Don't discriminate against black people." These and a variety of others are enforced by more sophisticated devices, mainly injunctions and orders.

Compensating for wrongs is another fairly simple purpose that came in early. In our system, it grew up as an alternative to punishing the wrongdoer, and it betrays its origin in ways that need not concern us here. But by now the procedures are both venerable and straightforward that enable a person injured through the negligence of another to recover money damages including medical expenses, and his loss of earnings through being unable to work. So are those that require a person who fails to live up to a contract to make good the loss sustained by the other party, or the profit he would have made had the contract been kept.

Only a little younger and slightly more complex are the devices for making a person disgorge what he has come by unfairly or dishonestly, or turn over the profits from overreaching other people. Here we use money judgments for such things as unjust enrichment or money paid by mistake, and we use injunctions to compel a person to give up documents he has tricked or coerced someone into signing, or property he has bought with another's money in his own name.

Lately, we have been expanding into more difficult realms. For instance, we are extending money damages to cover pain and suffering, injury to feelings, and even wrongful death. Sometimes there is an element of punishment here. If I behave outrageously enough when I wrong you, you will even recover an item of damages labelled punitive. But in many cases there is a real attempt to use cash to compensate for more or less inchoate harms. The problem is that things like the ridicule of one's friends and acquaintances, the loss of sexual function, or the loss of a leg by a writer or a business executive, while real enough harms, differ from out of pocket expenses, or loss of earnings and profits in having no ascertainable money equivalent. Plaintiffs' attorneys, much to the annoyance of opposing counsel, have developed a scheme for turning this fact into astronomical recoveries for their clients. Say a middle-aged man has lost his right leg. By standard mortality tables he has twenty-five years to live. "Would you," his attorney asks the jury, "be willing to accept two dollars a day for your right leg? Surely, two dollars a day is not too much to ask for a loss like that. Two multiplied by twenty-five multiplied by

365 equals 18,250: a more than fair amount to ask for this item of damage." Rather than face this kind of argument, a defendant recently settled with a twenty-one-year old quadriplegic for a million dollars.

It is hard to begrudge the young man his money, and certainly no one would want to trade places with him. But there is obviously a difference between putting right a harm that has been done and paying great sums of money on account of a harm that cannot be put right. I suppose what we are trying to do when we make payments like this is, first, to make the sufferer as comfortable as we can in the only way possible, and, second, to affirm symbolically his worth and our respect for him. The general purpose of this kind of relief should perhaps be described not as compensation but as salvage. The object (whether or not this is a good way of achieving it) is not so much to make up for the harm as to improve the overall situation the harm has brought about.

The idea of salvage has penetrated a number of situations in which the law formerly gave relief for more limited purposes. Take the case of divorce. Originally, the idea was that a wife or husband who had been the victim of certain matrimonial offenses was legally entitled to be free of the offending spouse. Hence the basic relief of a judgment declaring the marriage to be at an end. Ancillary to this were appropriate orders on such matters as alimony or division of jointly owned property. These were based on legal rights, such as that of the wife to be supported by the husband, that had existed during the marriage, and had not been forfeited by any matrimonial offense. But modern courts have departed from the traditional approach. First they began affording alimony to a wife on occasion even though she was not technically innocent. Then they began giving her a share in property that was not technically hers. They justified themselves by looking beyond the legal relations of the parties to the personal ones, and considering the whole history of the marriage instead of the immediate congeries of guilt and offenses. From there it was but a step to framing relief in such a way as to reorder as well as possible the whole human situation brought about by the marriage and its dissolution. Currently, legislatures are beginning to complement the judicial initiative by providing *no-fault* divorce laws, in which an "irretrievable breakdown of the marriage," a situation in need of salvage, is sufficient for relief, without a showing of specific misconduct.

This shift in the focus of relief from enforcing specific obligations and redressing specific harms to salvaging total situations is not limited to personal and domestic matters. For instance, in the realm of business the traditional device of selling off the assets of an insolvent debtor and dividing the proceeds pro rata among the creditors has been replaced in great part by corporate reorganization, a proceeding devoted to developing and implementing a plan to keep the business running for the creditors' benefit. Similarly, in enforcing the anti-trust laws, we do not simply put down illegal practices: we frame elaborate orders aimed at establishing viable competing units in the business involved.

Here, salvage for the past shades into prevention for the future. Injunctions against anticipated wrongs are another traditional form of relief; they are related to the cry of Haro under the Dukes of Normandy. Generally, you can have an injunction if you can show that someone is about to do you a legal wrong that money damages will not adequately redress. Other forms of relief for similar purposes are peace bonds — if a person is threatening to beat you up, you can make him put up a sum of money to be forfeited if he breaks the peace — appointment of guardians for people who cannot take care of their money, and commitment to institutions of people who will be dangerous if left at large. Here again, the trend in more complicated cases is to deal with the whole situation rather than limit relief to preventing specific wrongs.

PUNISHMENT

The punishing of wrongdoers is another of the most primitive functions of a legal system. Its origin lies in the legendary past, with rulers or elders moving first to regulate, then to supersede, the exaction of private vengeance. But now that the desire for private vengeance has come to be denounced by moralists as unworthy, by utilitarians as counterproductive, by believers in progress as barbaric, we have no small difficulty explaining why we keep on punishing people — although very few of us are minded to stop.

Of the philosophical justifications offered, the first in point of time is the retributive. The idea is that a criminal, having exercised more liberty than is proper to him must now be made to exercise less, so that the metaphysical balance between what is and what is not subject to his will may be restored. Even if this is good metaphysics, it is not easy to see what legitimate purpose of government it serves.

The punishment theory most favored among utilitarians is that of deterrence. People refrain from committing crimes because the pain they anticipate in being punished outweighs the pleasure they expect from committing a crime or enjoying the fruits of it. Clearly, as to certain crimes — rape, intrafamily homicides, drunkeness — this is bad psychology. If we do things like this, we do them under emotional pressure, and pretty much without counting the cost. With other offenses, however, the approach is perfectly sound. An antitrust violator, a swindler, or a person who parks in a no-parking zone calculates pretty closely what he has to gain against what he has to lose, and will be very apt to be deterred if the punishment is severe enough and likely enough to be imposed.

The most telling objection to the deterrent theory is not practical but philosophical. The pursuit of deterrence severs the relation between the punishment and the crime. It is not the punishment but the threat of it that deters. When a crime has been committed, the law has already failed in its purpose with respect to that crime; we impose the punishment only to give credibility to the threat for another time. This purpose has no necessary connection with the person being punished. To be sure, we may stop him from committing the same crime again, but the main idea is to stop other people. Punishment thus conceived seems to violate the moral principle that bids us recognize every human being as having value in himself, and forbids us to deal with him for a purpose entirely extraneous to him. We can argue of course that it is for the good of the whole community to have crime deterred, and since the person being punished is part of the community, the punishment is not for a purpose extraneous to him. But this proves too much: it would justify punishing not only people who commit crimes but people who are suspected of doing so. The deterrent effect of punishing suspects without trial is amply demonstrated in many a totalitarian regime. If this kind of punishment is unjust, it must be because punishment needs some additional justification besides the fact that it makes the deterrent good.

A very popular theory of punishment these days is the rehabilitative. According to this theory, we assume custody of criminals in order to provide them with the conditioning necessary to turn them into useful and law-abiding members of society. In this way, we can justify punishing people by saying it is for their own good. There is no doubt that some of our treatment of some types of offenders is in accordance with this theory: our indeterminate sentences, our systems of probation and parole, our efforts, such as they are, at counselling and vocational training of prisoners. On the other hand, some aspects of punishment would be very hard to square with the theory. It is hard to see, for instance, how a fine rehabilitates anyone.

Furthermore, our handling of infractions by the police belies any general rehabilitative intent in our criminal law. A person can be demonstrably guilty of a crime, and yet escape punishment because the police acted illegally in gathering the evidence of his guilt. On the rehabilitative theory, this means he can be deprived of rehabilitation he clearly needs because the police wronged him in discovering that he needed it. Now, suppose the police broke into a man's home without a warrant, found him in a coma on the floor, and rushed him to the hospital. It would be a bizarre legal system that made them put him back because they had acted illegally in learning of his condition. But if you adhere strictly to the rehabilitative theory, our own system is just as bizarre.

Also inconsistent with the rehabilitative theory is our treatment of crimes committed by the mentally ill. In such cases, the defendant is found not guilty, and assigned to some kind of treatment, which we insist is not a punishment. If punishment were itself a form of treatment, the distinction would be meaningless.

Finally, the rehabilitative theory fails to explain why we limit our punishments to those who commit crimes. Obviously, a potential criminal is as much in need of rehabilitation as a person who has already committed a crime, and he will probably be easier to rehabilitate. Yet, however persuasive the sociological and psychological data indicating that a certain person is apt to commit crimes, we consider it unjust to subject him to compulsory rehabilitation when he has not in fact done anything wrong. Even our traditional procedures for commitment of the mentally ill, though they are sharply distinguished from criminal proceedings, worry us a good deal. The only rehabilitative programs that leave us fairly comfortable are those like the sexual psycopath laws that are set in motion by conviction of a specific crime.

One other theory that seems worth considering is that of incapacitation: by imprisoning the criminal or putting him to death, we take him out of circulation and thus put an end to his crimes. This too has some basis in reality. Any law enforcement official probably has a select list of people he would dearly love to put away for the protection of the community. But the general principles of criminal law offer him little encouragement. Courts generally feel that a person should be punished for what he has done, not for what he is going to do. While the likelihood of further crimes is certainly taken into account in imposing sentence, it is not, and could not be, a sufficient guide. Life imprisonment of an incorrigible petty thief, or even of an incorrigible reckless driver, would be considered unjust; so would letting a man off scot free who has poisoned a wealthy aunt, and thereby acquired enough money to live comfortably without having to murder anyone ever again. There is even a certain amount of protest against letting a man's general reputation as a leader of organized crime influence the zeal with which he is prosecuted or the severity with which he is punished for income tax evasion.

To sort out all these theories and their objections, we might begin by distinguishing between the purpose of punishment and the justification for it. The theories of deterrence, rehabilitation, and incapacitation all state purposes that we can and do pursue in punishing a person once we have decided that he is a fit subject for punishment. But the fact that one or more of these purposes can profitably be served in his case does not by itself make him such a fit subject. Nor does the fact that none of these purposes will be served entitle him to escape punishment. That a person has done something wrong seems to be both a necessary and a sufficient condition for punishing him justly.

Of the theories we have considered, only the retributive offers an account of why this should be the case. That account, as I suggested earlier, seems inadequate. The metaphysical basis for restricting a person's liberty on one occasion because he has exceeded it on another is no more apparent than the metaphysical basis for slicing off his ears because his nose is too long. It is all very well to pursue harmony and balance, but they are not as easily come by as this. Nor is it apparent why harmony and balance on a metaphysical level should be a concern of government. The authority of government to intervene in people's affairs is generally supposed to depend on some practical purpose to be achieved by doing so, either the good of the whole community, or that of the person affected. It may be that the maintenance of metaphysical harmony is good for people, but the traditional basis of the theory is harmony for its own sake: it would have to be stated in a new way to give it a practical purpose.

Then, to develop a persuasive principle of retribution we must either clarify or replace the traditional formula. In trying to do so, we will not get much help from modern authors. Many of them do admit retribution to a place in their schemes of punishment, either as a personal intuition or as a concession to a deep-seated popular prejudice, but they do not concern themselves much with its theoretical basis. The nearest thing to a theory that any of them have advanced is that retribution expresses the community's moral condemnation of the crime. On this view, punishment is a device for social orientation like those discussed earlier. Retribution thus understood becomes an additional purpose of punishment rather than a justification for it. The theory leaves untouched the fundamental question which a sound retributive theory must answer: Why is it right to achieve a given purpose by inflicting pain or frustration on a person who has done wrong, when it is not right to achieve the same purpose by inflicting the same pain or frustration on a person who has not?

I find an answer in looking at crime and punishment in the light of what they have in common, the exercise of power. The criminal has exercised an unjust power, a power to which he is not entitled, over a specific victim, over the community in general, or at least over his own affairs. In punishing him, the government, on behalf of the community — or on behalf of God, if you follow St. Paul — exercises a just power over him. What the punishment restores is not the abstract metaphysical balance between what is and what is not subject to the will of the criminal, but a highly concrete superiority of just over unjust power.

At the beginning of this work, I spoke of vindication against unjust power as one of the two basic claims people have always made on their legal systems. I suggested that from my own religious standpoint the claim is related to God's primordial promise to go on ruling the world. But whether or not it is adequately grounded in Genesis, the manifestation that where unjust power is at work, a just and stronger power is also at work plays a vital part in man's orientation toward the world in which he lives. On one level, crime is a misfortune like any other. Being mugged and relieved of twenty-five dollars is no more painful or costly than slipping on a banana peel and paying twenty-five dollars for X-rays. Being shot is no more fatal than a heart attack, a burglary no more destructive than a fire. A crime wave disrupts a community less than an epidemic or a flash flood. But in each case the effect on human beings is quite different. Crime requires not simply an adjustment to misfortune, but a reconsideration of the kind of world in which we have supposed we were living. Instead of being subject to impersonal forces that operate according to their own intrinsic logic, whether it be to our benefit or to our detriment, we find we are subject to a personal malevolence that we did nothing to bring on and can do nothing to call off. The solemn moral condemnation of the person who has wronged us, coupled with an exercise of power over him — the two elements essential to any true criminal process — have in this context an effect of reassurance: they proclaim that while malevolent powers are at work, they are not the dominant powers in the world. This reassurance operates to return the crime to the level of a common misfortune, instead of a disorienting experience of the world.

Retribution understood in this way meets the two objections I put to the traditional formula. It makes what is done to the criminal commensurate with what he himself has done: since both are exercises of power, one can be set off against the other. It serves a purpose of government, because it operates to the good of the community, the victim, and the criminal himself, all of whom need for their orientation in life a true understanding of the relation between power and justice in the world in which they live.

In the light of this need, it would be well to take another look at the much-maligned desire for vengeance, the historical foundation of the whole criminal law. The moralists and philosophers who condemn this desire have advanced remarkably little in the way of solid argument to support their case against it. They have certainly not sustained the heavy burden of proof that ought to rest on anyone who condemns out of hand something this deeply rooted in human experience. Other primordial vices — lust, greed, avarice — are not condemned as wholly unworthy motivations, but as perverted or inordinate versions of worthy ones. There is nothing inherently wrong with wanting to make love, to eat, to save money: the vice is in wanting to do these things too much or in the wrong way. By analogy, it ought to be possible to separate the vice of *vindictiveness*, the perverted or inordinate desire for vengeance, from the legitimate desire for *vindication*, a just retribution upon those who have wronged us. It seems to me our desire is legitimate if we seek nothing more than an effective reaffirmation of the superiority of just over unjust power in our lives. It is a perversion if we seek to exact a retribution disproportionate to the wrong, or if we try to establish the superiority of just over unjust power in our lives. It is a perversion if we seek to exact a retribution disproportionate to the wrong, or if we try to establish the superiority of an unjust power favorable to our purposes over a just power that has thwarted us.

If I am right, it would seem that the victim of a crime has a just claim to be vindicated, which is distinct from the claim of the community to punish the offender. It is a claim that has scant recognition these days. There are to be sure a few survivals of an earlier concern with the victim: in some cases by statute or by the custom of police and prosecutors a criminal will get off if his victim does not want him punished; conversely, the defense of entrapment by the police will probably not be accepted if there is a specific victim hurt by the crime. But most of the time both the theory and the practice of the criminal law proceed on the assumption that only the community has an interest in the punishment of crime.

This assumption enters into discretionary decisions like when to accept a plea or how severely to punish. It is beginning to affect the drafting and codification of criminal statues. Most of all, it is reflected in the growing body of judicial decisions releasing criminals when the community's law enforcement machinery has operated unfairly in bringing them to book. Obviously, the fact that the evidence against a man was illegally obtained does not make it less likely that he committed the crime of which he was accused. Nor in most cases does the fact that he was indicted by an improperly selected jury, or that his trial was unreasonably delayed. In cases of this kind, the object of the courts is not so much to protect the accused against being convicted of something he did not do as to control the agents of the community in the investigation and trial of crimes. This is fair enough if only the community is concerned. But it is hard on the victim if he has a just claim to his vindication — which he must perforce leave to the agents of the community even if they botch it.

I am not prepared to say how heavily we should weigh this claim of the victim against the other values we try to pursue in ordering the criminal process. I only suggest that we cannot answer the question by ignoring it. I think this lack of attention to the victim is behind a great deal of the inarticulate discontent that many people feel with current developments in criminal procedure. This discontent is out of proportion to the effect any of these developments has on crime as a potential misfortune. It may well be that I am more likely to be mugged than I was ten years ago, but I doubt if the fact that the police need a warrrant to recover the loot has a great deal to do with this state of affairs. I think what bothers people is not so much that there are more crimes (you are still in much more danger of an automobile accident than of a crime, and you probably worry about it a good deal less) as that the just power that ought to be raised in their vindication seems to be artificially stayed.

Another place where I think the victim's claim needs more attention, though again I am not sure how much weight it should have, is in the debate over the abolition of capital punishment. On the utilitarian level where most of this debate takes place, there is really very little to argue. Obviously, the death penalty rehabilitates, if at all, only in an eschatological sense. While it might deter some crimes, for instance antitrust violations, fairly well, it seems no better than other forms of punishment in deterring the crimes to which it is customarily applied: the homicide rate does not vary significantly between states that do and states that do not inflict it. It does prevent recidivism, but recidivism is very low among murderers punished in other ways. Finally, even if it did serve some major utilitarian purpose, utility simply is not a sufficient justification for killing people.

If I hesitate to accept these arguments in favor of abolition, it is because I do not feel they reach the real problem. That problem as I see it is whether any alternative punishment can afford an adequate vindication to those persons whose lives have been touched by an unjust exercise of the power of life and death. That power is surely the most awesome that one human being can exercise over another. If the state renounces it, it will become the exclusive prerogative of criminals. We have yet to discover how people's orientation toward the world will be affected by a general awareness that this has happened.

III

INSTITUTIONS
The Formal Cause

6

FORMALITY AND JUSTICE

LAW ABOUT LAW

A number of stories in the *Arabian Nights* have the Caliph wandering through the streets of Baghdad in disguise, conversing with his subjects, and meting out summary rewards and punishments on the basis of what he finds out in the process. This is one way of using the available means of social control, and in the circumstances of the stories it produces at least poetic justice. But it seems too offhand to pass muster as law. We may say that by the legal norms of the *Arabian Nights* the word of the Caliph is law, but we do not quite believe it. We would like him to pronounce his word in some special place, to have it written down in some special way, to warn us in advance of what he is going to have to say about our affairs, to listen to us with certain kinds of solemnity: in short, to exercise his authority under institutional forms. The collectivity of such forms I call the formal cause of the legal order. An order that lacks them falls short of being legal in the way a used palette falls short of being a painting, a love affair of being a marriage, or a stack of lumber of being a house.

Many of the dispositions of any legal system are concerned with establishing and ordering these forms. Examples cover a wide range of familiar topics: how a bill in the legislature becomes law, what cases are in the jurisdiction of what court, when a contract must be in writing, how many witnesses you need for a will, when an agent can bind his principal. Historically, this kind of law about law seems to precede and control the other dispositions of a legal system — let us call them law about people. A society in a stage we would characterize as prelegal has already its characteristic notions of how people are expected to behave, and of what to do about people who behave otherwise. The first venture of such a society into the realm of law is the establishment of devices for routinely and peaceably bringing these notions to bear on situations that arise. It is only the experience of these devices in operation that creates a need for further devices to restate or modify the underlying notions.

Thus, in our own legal system, when Henry II commissioned his judges to impose a common law on the polymorphous institutions and expectations that prevailed in his realm, he did not find it necessary to tell them what that law was to be. That they took where they found it. They examined charters and documents. They interrogated panels of citizens about local customs and rights in land. They applied principles of Christian theology. They dragged out snippets of learning in Roman and canon law. It was only after they had had a chance to experience specific inadequacies in all this material that they began bringing it into what later became Parliament for restatement and revision.

A great deal of what the early judges had to decide concerned the scope of their authority — neither who ought to prevail in this case nor what ought to be done for him, but whether the case was one the king had assigned this particular set of judges to hear. Cases were still coming up where the expectations of the community were not routinely met by any institutional form the system had yet devised. Some of these cases became the subject of legislation like the great Statute of Westminster II (1285). Others the king referred to ad hoc tribunals (commissions of oyer and terminer) or to his Chancellor, who developed routines of his own for handling them, and so built up our system of equity.

I would say it was not until the seventeenth century that the English legal enterprise became more concerned with clarifying or modifying what people were expected to do, and with devising more sophisticated ways of dealing with failure to live up to expectations than it was with ordering and refining its own institutional forms. With the resolution of the disputes between Crown and Parliament, between lay and ecclesiastical courts, between common-law courts and Chancery, the institutional structure became pretty well fixed, and judges, commentators, and legislators alike devoted themselves with renewed zeal and creativity to restating the substantive law, the law about people, and modifying it to meet new needs. The law continued to develop in this way until the late nineteenth or early twentieth century, when the growth of administrative agencies and an increased concern for the rights of criminal defendants began bringing institutional questions again to the fore.

RULES, RIGHTS, AND REMEDIES

In reviewing this history, I have treated the question of how people are expected to behave and the question of what to do about people who behave otherwise as parallel objects of institutional concern. Institutional responses to these two questions are the two aspects of social control that I handled in the last two chapters. Setting forth an expectation in the form of a rule or principle is one way of getting people to live up to it; imposing some kind of consequence or sanction on their not doing so is another. I regard these means of social control as collectively constituting the matter of law, while the institutions through which they are developed and applied are the form. In stressing this division of matter and form, I give less importance than most authors do to the difference between the two kinds of social control. Their tendency is to see the treatment of noncompliance, the remedies or sanctions, as pertaining to form, process, law about law, while only the formulated standards of behavior constitute law about people.

It is not on merely metaphysical grounds that I have departed from the customary categories of analysis: I find as a practical matter that they do not offer a satisfactory account of legal institutions and how they work. Separating social control from standards of behavior obscures the unity and flexibility of the law's total response to the life of the community, while lumping social controls with institutions obscures the important differences between the problem of developing effective institutions and the problem of choosing appropriate social controls. To illustrate, let us look at a couple of standard approaches to one of the classic problems of jurisprudence, the right-remedy problem.

The problem is this: Does the law apply a remedy because someone in authority has discerned a right, or does it speak of a right because someone in authority has resolved on applying a remedy? Will the sheriff put you off my land because it is mine, or do we say it is mine because the sheriff will put you off? Despite its appearance, the problem is not merely academic. It crops up in a number of cases where someone tries to extend a standard remedy to a new right, or a new remedy to a standard right. If a union contract gives an employee a grievance, can he go to court when the grievance procedure fails him? When a judgment in an automobile accident case is discharged under the federal Bankruptcy Act, may a state suspend your driver's license for not paying it? If a court is abolished, what happens to the rights it used to enforce? Does a moratorium on mortgage foreclosures violate the United States Consitution by "impairing the obligations" or mortgages? In one way or another, all these questions depend on how you handle the right-remedy problem.

Hart exemplifies one of the prevailing approaches. He is quite clear that the right is logically prior to the remedy, and can indeed exist without it. Rights for him are created by primary rules, rules which impose obligations on people (do this or don't do that). If such a rule requires *Y* to do or abstain from something at *X*'s behest, then it can be said that in the legal system to which that rule belongs, *X* has a right. Remedies belong to what Hart calls secondary rules. These are his rules of law about law; he distinguishes them sharply from his primary rules, which is law about people. A complete legal system for him is constituted by a union of the two types of rules, the secondary controlling the identification (rules of recognition); development (rules of change); and application (rules of adjudication) of the primary.

The presuppositions of Hart's analysis seem to be these:

1. Law about people is concerned with providing an authoritative model for specific aspects of human behavior.
2. Law about law is concerned with constructing, improving, and using the model.

The first of these is the common position of Analytical Positivists. By supplementing it with the second, Hart is able to meet the contemporary demand for a sophisticated treatment of law about law, and yet leave the essential positivist tradition intact. This is no mean accomplishment, but it can rise no higher than the positivist tradition itself. I have already indicated what my objection to that tradition is: in my opinion, there is no self-contained legal model of human behavior. Rather, the expectations of which the law takes account emerge from the ongoing life of the community through a process of dialogue in which the law plays a part, but only a part.

Here is an example of what I mean. *A* goes hunting along the beach with a shotgun. Finding a pleasant rock by the sea, he lies down on it and falls asleep. When he wakes up, he is cut off by the tide. As he cannot swim, he is afraid he will drown when the tide rises higher. Just then, *B*, *A*'s worst enemy, comes along in a rowboat. *A* asks to be rowed ashore. *B* refuses, stating that it will give him great pleasure to watch *A* drown. But *A* levels his shotgun at *B*, threatening to shoot unless *B* rows him ashore. *B* complies under protest, and, upon coming to shore, has *A* arrested for assault with a deadly weapon.

It is a commonplace among first-year law students, and their teachers, that *B*, although he may have had a moral obligation to rescue *A*, had no legal obligation to do so. Hart would put it that there is in the Anglo-American legal system no primary rule calling on *B* to rescue *A*, or giving *A* a legal right to be rescued. Furthermore, by the rules usually recognized in the system, I am not allowed to use a threat of deadly force to compel a person to do something unless he has a legal obligation to do it. But despite this adverse state of the rules, it is clear as a practical matter that *A* would not be convicted of the assault. The reason he would not be convicted is that everyone would think *B* ought to have rescued him. Even if there is not a legal obligation to rescue, the law will not be oblivious of the moral obligation to do so. The law takes account of whatever expectations it finds current in the life of the community, even if they have not been previously embodied in legal rules.

But if the law will take notice of the obligation to rescue, in what sense can it be said not to be a legal obligation? Only in the sense that the failure to rescue is neither a tort nor a crime in most cases. I may of course have overlooked other ways in which the obligation to rescue is not treated like other obligations, but it does not matter. What is important is that the relevant statements about there being or not being a legal obligation to rescue are not statements about models of human behavior, but statements about the sanctions with which standards of behavior generally accepted in the community are or are not enforced. If you do not have a full-fledged legal right to be rescued, it is for lack of a remedy, not for lack of a rule.

The idea of founding rights on the existence of remedies is central to the major American contribution to this kind of analysis, the *Hohfeldian* system, originated early in this century by Professor W. N. Hohfeld. He and his followers articulated the whole law in terms of eight legal relations, four concerned with law about people, the other four with law about law. The system is elegant, with each relation having an opposite and a correlative among the others. The four relations dealing with law about people are *right, duty, privilege,* and *no right.* Right and duty, privilege and no right are correlatives. Duty and privilege, right and no right are opposites. The terms are used this way. If the law gives me a remedy against *X* in case he does not do so-and-so, then he owes me a *duty* to do it, and I have a *right* that he shall. But if the law gives me no remedy against him, then, as far as I am concerned, he has a *privilege* not to do it, and I have *no right* that he shall. Note that he does not have a *right* not to do it unless the law will go further and give him a remedy in case I try to make him.

With these tools, we can handle the problem of the hunter on the rock better than we could with Hart's set. Since the law will give *A* no remedy if *B* fails to rescue him, *B* has a privilege not to, or no duty to, and *A* has no right that he shall. But since the law will give *B* no remedy if he is compelled to effect the rescue, he does not have a right not to do it; rather, *A* has a privilege to compel him. Unless (it is a big unless, but let it pass) self-help is regarded as some kind of a remedy afforded by law, this analysis takes care of the case.

But with other cases it is not so easy. Suppose, for instance, your wife goes home to her mother. In most states, if you have not done anything to drive her away, the law will give you a remedy. It will impose various financial burdens on her. In due course, it will find her guilty of desertion, and grant you a divorce or a separation. Since these remedies are available, it seems that you have a right for her to come back, and she has a duty to do so. On the other hand, if you bring her home by force, and hold her there, a court will issue a writ of habeas corpus and command you to release her. It follows that she has a right to leave, since the law will give her a remedy if you make her stay. But to say that she has at once a right to leave and a duty to return is to make nonsense of the whole analysis.

Or consider a Fair Housing Law, which purports to give a would-be home buyer a right not to be discriminated against on account of his race. Typically, such laws are enforced by a Civil Rights Commission, using a lengthy administrative process of conciliation plus gradually increasing application of force. As an alternative to invoking that remedy, such as it is, may a black man physically resist the real estate developer who tries to eject him from a model home he is looking at (generally, he has a privilege to defend himself against someone who tries to put him out of a place where he has a right to be)? May the State Real Estate Commission revoke the license of a broker who discriminates (assume his license is subject to revocation if he breaches a duty to a buyer)? It makes a good deal more sense to answer questions like these by examining the moral and social background of the law than by analyzing the Hohfeldian rights or privileges of the parties.

Where the Hohfeldian system goes wrong, it seems to me, is in trying to look at whether the law does or does not afford a remedy, and ignoring the possibility that the law may afford one remedy and withhold others. This is all very well when you are looking at standard remedies that generallly come in familiar bundles, but when you are looking at extraordinary or newfangled remedies, it breaks down. For this reason, the Hohfeldian analysis cannot afford a complete solution to the right-remedy problem, still less a general account of the law.

In the light of these criticisms of other people's theories, let us look at my definition of a right. I said in an earlier chapter that "*X* has a right" means that X has a stake in other people's conduct, which, upon colorably rational grounds, the government will expect the community to recognize, and the community will expect the government to enforce. As I have tried to show in a number of places, the expectations involved in this formula arise out of a dialogue between government and community, or between the legal enterprise and the ongoing life of the community it regulates. They do not arise, therefore, from a model intrinsic to the legal enterprise. That is the basis of my objection to Hart.

The enforcement expected of the government in the formula involves the application of any of the means of social control considered in the last two chapters. The adoption of a rule or principle with the moral force of the law behind it is just as surely a kind of enforcement as the application of a remedy in the strict sense. The decision to apply social controls for a given purpose leaves room for a great deal of flexibility in choosing which ones to apply. It is the failure to allow this flexibility that constitutes my objection to the Hohfeldian system.

In my own scheme of analysis, a social convention or moral claim is transformed into a legal right when government and community concur in recognizing it as a suitable one for the application of social control. Its recognition by the agencies of government, its institutionalization, gives it the form of a legal right. Its promulgation in a form that invokes the community's willingness to "obey the law" is already enough of a social control to provide the matter of a legal right. Once the legal right has been established, the adoption of more specific formulations and the adoption of more effective remedies are both technical matters of choosing appropriate social controls. Thus, in the rescue case, your right to be rescued is recognized in a number of ways as a legal one in that legislators and text writers are continually taxing their ingenuity to find means of social control that will suitably support it. Most of them think the standard sanctions of tort and crime are not suitable, mainly, I suspect, because of the difficulty of identifying who has the duty to rescue, and determining to what lengths he must go. But proposals for rewards, and indirect motivations (for instance compensation for losses incurred) are continually being mooted and in some cases accepted. It is against this background that we find it easy to allow the person who needs to be rescued the privilege of self-help. Similarly, we have no difficulty saying that your wife has a duty to live with you even though there are cogent reasons for not enforcing that duty through physical restraints. Finally, in the case of the Fair Housing Act, we can say that the legislation created a legal right not to be discriminated against because it finally recognized that the moral principle on the subject was an appropriate one for enforcing with social controls. Once we say this, we can evaluate on its own merits the case for giving the right further enforcement through the application of social controls not specifically mentioned in the legislation.

INSTITUTIONAL JUSTICE

It is through institutional forms and processes that expectations are recognized and clarified and that social controls are developed and applied. We like to think that the aim of all this activity is a just ordering of the ongoing life of the community — substantive justice, let us call it. But that is only part of the story. It is not enough to achieve just results: the work as it goes forward must be justly done. Institutions are subject to a kind of institutional justice that deals with their internal functioning, as distinguished from their end results. The principles of institutional justice, embodied in Latin tags, and consecrated by the learning of ancient authors, are part of the folklore of the legal profession. They represent centuries of experience in operating old institutions and building new ones. They not only go beyond the achievement of substantive justice; they often militate actively against it. Let us look at a representative sample of them; then we can consider how the whole subject fits into the general quest for justice.

First, here are four principles that might be called constitutive. They deal with how institutions are established and what they are supposed to do.

Rex non potest peccare — The king can do no wrong. This does not mean that whatever the king does is right. Quite the opposite: it means that whatever wrong he does is not done in his official capacity, and therefore has no legal effect. It follows of course that his orders cannot justify anyone else in doing wrong. No institution can operate free from external moral restraint. The power to do wrong does not reside in the system: no one can assign it, and no one can receive it.

Delegata potestas non potest delegari — A delegated power cannot be delegated. The judge cannot set his former law partner to hearing cases for him while he goes fishing. The policeman cannot send his brother-in-law to arrest you. Officials may have the power to appoint deputies, but only if that power is given them by law. This is not the most important, but probably the least complicated of a number of principles supporting the rule of law. The power given one person over another must be specific, limited, and structured; it is not to be handed about at whim.

Ubi jus ibi remedium — Where there is a right there is a remedy. This is the view I have taken of the right-remedy problem. It was already old in 1703, when Chief Justice Holt applied it in the famous case of *Ashby v. White*. The plaintiff was allowed to maintain a standard tort action against an election official who kept him from voting, even though no remedy had been given in such a case before, and even though the candidate he would have voted for was elected.

Potior est conditio defendentis – The defendant has the stronger case. The plaintiff has the burden of pleading and proving his case. If the court is in irremediable doubt, the defendant will prevail. If neither party is entitled to a piece of property, the one who has it will keep it. If the parties are both blameworthy (*in pari delicto*), neither can recover against the other. You are innocent until proven guilty. You may do what you please unless someone can point to a specific reason for stopping you. In most cases, you are not liable for negligence unless the person complaining was taking due care. All this expresses what might be called the inertia of a legal system. Law is a ponderous and awesome mechanism. There is a burden of persuasion on the person who wants to set it in motion, a presumption in favor of the person who wants to leave it at rest.

Next, here are three procedural principles. They govern how the apparatus goes about reaching results.

Audi alteram partem – Hear the other side. Barring emergencies (someone about to tear down a building, burn the evidence, skip the state), you do not intervene in another person's affairs until you have heard what he has to say for himself. If you are a judge, you hold a trial. If you are an administrator, you hold some kind of formal hearing, the scope and procedures depending on the nature of the matter in hand. If you are a legislator, you try at the very least to consider informally the arguments advanced by those affected by a proposed law. This is fundamental. In the first place, the person you are dealing with usually knows more about his own affairs than anyone else does: he may be able to help you reach a just decision. But even if you were well enough informed in some other way, you would still have to listen to him. Your intervention entails a human relation, and a human relation entails dialogue.

Nemo judex in causa sua – No one may be judge in his own case. From this principle flow the rigorously chaste Canons of Judicial Ethics, the amorphous inhibitions about buying drinks for administrators, the raised eyebrows when government officials quit and go to work at high salaries for the people they used to regulate, the concern over part-time legislators with outside jobs. Here again, it is a matter of utility plus something more. Naturally, human nature being what it is, we are more apt to get a just decision from someone who has no personal stake in the outcome. But beyond that, it is important to the dialogue in which law is articulated that one who speaks with the authority of law appear as the representative of that authority and nothing else.

Interest reipublicae ut finis sit litium — It is for the general welfare that there be an end to litigation. We have statutes of limitations to prevent the raking up of old claims. We have rules of res judicata and collateral estoppel to prevent the reconsideration of matters already considered once and disposed of. We have rules of compulsory joinder and rules against interlocutory appeals so that controversies can be disposed of all at once instead of piecemeal. We have a constitutional doctrine that an accused cannot be twice put in jeopardy for one offense. We have (or ought to have) procedures for speeding up trials and keeping lawsuits from dragging out. Being sued or accused is traumatic. For the sake of the defendant, we want it over and done with as soon as possible. For the sake of the plaintiff also, we want to move to a quick decision. If he needs the law's help, he needs it right away. In the words of New Jersey's great procedural innovator, the late Chief Justice Vanderbilt, "justice delayed is justice denied."

Finally, here are three formulative principles, affecting the relation between formulation and application, the general and the particular, in the exercise of institutional authority.

Nulla poena sine lege — No punishment without a law. We forbid ex post facto legislation, which makes something a crime after you have done it, or makes the penalty more severe than it was when you did it. We forbid legislation that defines crimes so vaguely that you cannot be sure whether you are committing them or not, for instance charging "unreasonable" prices or being a "member of a gang." On analogous principles, we discourage retrospective legislation which alters civil consequences after the event, or legislation which imposes unpleasant civil consequences so vaguely that you cannot figure out how to avoid them. Law is a matter of expectations, and you are entitled to know what the expectations are: what is expected of you, and what you can expect of the government. There is a debate over whether natural law, morality, or other generally accepted norms of conduct can occupy the place of written law in the application of this maxim. For instance, a number of jurists have objected to the Nuremberg war crimes trials on the ground that there was no law that condemned what the defendants did at the time they did it, whereas other jurists have insisted that the defendants ought on general principles to have known that what they were doing was wrong. Needless to say, my sympathies are with the second group.

Cessante ratione cessat ipsa lex — Where the reason ceases, the law itself ceases. There is an old case under a statute requiring a train to stop when an animal or obstruction appeared on the track. A farmer was suing a railroad company because one of its trains had run over three of his geese without stopping. The court held that the statute was meant to secure the safety of the train and its passengers, and did not apply to an animal too small to endanger the train. The point is that legal formulations are a product of human intelligence reflecting on the life of the community in which they are introduced. Since language is never fully adequate to thought, or thought to reality, such formulas cannot be taken for autonomous verbalisms, or cut loose from the purposive reflection that called them forth.

Summmum jus summa injuria — Extreme law is extreme wrong. There is a story of an immigration official in San Francisco who was puzzled about what to do when a woman got off a ship from China with a baby who had been born during the voyage. He wired his superiors in Washington asking whether he should send the baby back to China because it had no visa (the mother had one). They wired back "don't be a damned fool." I referred in an earlier chapter to a person who walks on the grass in the park in order to rescue a child from a dog. The ancient jurists talked about a law that required shutting the city gates at sundown, and said you did not have to apply it when the people of the surrounding countryside were fleeing into the city from an enemy. This is the principle of *epikeia*, an extension of the *cessante ratione* principle just discussed. It bids us limit legal formulas not only by their purposes but also by the whole life of the community: in short, apply them with discretion. Without discretion, they do not serve good purposes; they do great harm.

These ten of course are nothing like all the maxims there are: it would not be much trouble to fill a book with others of the same kind. But I think these will be sufficient to illustrate the basic requirements of institutional justice, and relate them to the other kinds of justice that institutions are supposed to secure.

The most important of these basic requirements is an awareness of limitations. No institution can accomplish fully what it is supposed to. It has only so much capacity for eliciting the relevant facts, still less for eliciting them quickly and accurately. The people running it have only so much of the wisdom, learning, virute, and stamina the job demands. Like any human device, it brings forth results only at the cost of time and effort, which may be disproportionate. Then, beyond all these circumstantial limitations are the fundamental limits of the human condition, the intractability of matter, the unpredictability of events, the inadequacy of thought and language, the ambivalence of history.

Faced with these limitations, a just institution intrudes only circumspectly into people's affairs. It restricts both its intake of business and its aspirations for handling that business to conform to its resources for gathering and weighing information. It maintains checks and balances so that one person's weaknesses may be set off by another's strengths. It does not choke its procedures or enervate its constituents in the pursuit of unattainable refinements on the rudimentary demands of justice and well-being. It has formal rules and procedures to keep its work from being distorted by the idiosyncrasies of people and events, but it applies them flexibly because they cannot take the full measure of what has to be done.

The romantic pursuit of ultimate justice in disregard of the available resources is a temptation to which most systems succumb on occasion, and some with regularity. The results are almost uniformly disastrous. Thus, while the medieval common law was developing its elaborate system of pleadings to bring forth a question that twelve peasants could answer yes or no and so dispose of the case, the canon law, with even less effective sources of information, was insisting that nothing was decided until it was decided right, and recording pages of testimony to be pored over by one panel of judges after another. Anyone who could took his lawsuit to the common law courts because it was next to impossible to get a final decision from the canonists as long as your opponent wanted to keep litigating. In our own century, we are familiar with what happened when people like Lenin, Trotsky, Mussolini, and Hitler ignored the procedural obstacles to solving the economic and social problems of their countries. Less familiar, but closer to home, are the cases where jurors are confined for weeks and months at a time lest outside influences lead them to confine a defendant unjustly, cases where tenants are so well protected against unjust eviction that landlords keep buildings vacant for years rather than rent them out and try to get them back when they need them for some other purpose, or cases where procedures for excluding undeserving welfare claimants are so rigorous that people do not dare go off welfare to get jobs because it is so hard to get back on again if they have to.

Related to the recognition that an institution has only a limited capacity for doing justice is the requirement that it operate predictably. If we cannot expect complete justice, we ought to know what we can expect. Hence the feeling that except in the most flagrant cases the requirements of the law should be set forth in writing before we get in trouble for violating them; the feeling that a decision, once reached, should be adhered to; the feeling that a court should not give judgment on a matter different from the one first pleaded, or against a bystander not a party to the case; the feeling that a government agency should have specific powers, rather than what Justice Cardozo called a "roving commission to inquire into evils, and, upon discovery, correct them."

Humanity, a final requirement of institutional justice, is also related to the inherent limitations of institutions. Man's thoughts are not God's thoughts nor his ways God's ways. Ultimate justice is not something one man bestows on another; it is something men pursue together. Lawyers, judges, legislators, administrators, jurors, witnesses, plaintiffs, defendants, accusers, accuseds, clerks, bailiffs, turnkeys, and even teachers and students of the law are all embarked on a common and arduous enterprise. It is essential to remember — and easy to forget — that no one involved is a cipher, datum, a problem, a pawn on the chessboard. Each is a participant in the process with a need and a voice of his own.

I mentioned that the requirements of institutional justice sometimes militate against institutions ordering with maximum justice the affairs they handle. It is easy enough to see why this is the case. When a new problem comes up, prompt action may be required to deal with it justly, whereas institutional justice is weighted in favor of deliberate action, or no action at all. When it is common knowledge that someone has committed a crime, a just ordering of society requires punishing him or redressing the wrong he has done; institutional justice requires giving him a fair trial — adequate notice, a chance to confront his accusers, a chance to be heard. Everyone has his favorite examples of "known" criminals who are running loose because no one has been able to gather the necessary resources to bring them to trial.

Everyone has also his favorite examples of kinds of behavior that ought to be prevented or people that ought to be taken care of or loopholes that ought to be closed which remain undealt with because institutional justice requires the standards for dealing with them to be formulated in advance, and no one is wise enough to formulate them or powerful enough to get his formulation through the legislative process. Looters of corporations, publishers of dirty books, evaders of income tax, incompetent schoolteachers, slum landlords, welfare recipients who spend their money on booze, and a host of others have sheltered from the sun of justice under this umbrella. In other cases, the wicked prosper because the close supervision necessary to find them out and stop them would burden the community unjustly. For instance, the Supreme Court, after considerable debate, has decided that it is better to let people maintain unsanitary conditions inside their houses than to require them to admit health inspectors on demand.

Then there are cases where institutional justice requires a just claim to be foregone because of the likelihood of an institution going wrong in trying to give it effect. The clearest example is the Statute of Frauds, which prevents certain contracts from being enforced unless they are evidenced by a writing. Genuine oral contracts must go unenforced lest the courts be deceived into enforcing spurious ones. By the same token, legitimate activities are often forbidden because the available institutions cannot effectively separate them from illegitimate ones. There was a time when yellow margarine fell under this principle; there may come a time when massage parlors do.

Somewhat the same principle seems to be involved in the current pressure to make employers hire a certain percentage of black people; there is no other way our institutions can adequately insure that blacks are not being discriminated against. It is argued in opposition that hiring a black man because he is black involves unjustly rejecting a white man because he is white. Prescinding from the question whether a black man should have special treatment to overcome the discrimination he has suffered in the past, the case would seem to be another of those in which institutional justice and substantive justice pull in opposite directions.

Of course, justice, like truth, is unitary. Particular considerations of justice may urge in opposite directions, but a whole course of action must be in the end either just or unjust. If institutional justice calls for one thing and substantive justice for another, the conflicting claims must be either balanced or resolved. Resolution is sometimes possible on the basis of a standard philosophical principle. For instance, since the end does not justify the means, you may not commit an institutional injustice in order to achieve a substantively just result — say by introducing perjured testimony to strengthen the evidence in favor of what you know to be the true facts, or (a favorite trick of medieval monasteries) forging charters to firm up your title to property you know is rightfully yours. Nor can you work a substantive injustice to make an institution operate justly — say by harassing witnesses in order to assure litigants a fair trial.

But in the greatest number of cases no philosophical priority can be established between the competing claims. Take the question of how much of a hearing you are entitled to before the sheriff repossesses your television set for the finance company. If there is no hearing, you will be subject to the indignity of having the sheriff barge into your living room without warning and make off with the set in the middle of your favorite program, all before there has been any official determination that you owe anything on it. If there is a hearing, you will have time while it is pending to hide the set in your garage or at your brother's house. The requirement of institutional justice, *audi alteram partem*, may run counter to the requirement of substantive justice, *suum cuique dedere*, give to each what is his.

But this time it is not a question of justice in one category being purchased at the price of injustice in the other. If the proceedings are drawn out to the point that the set can no longer be found, they can be called ineffective, but not unjust. The institution has not produced a substantive injustice; it has merely failed in its task of correcting one. Pragmatic, not philosophical, priorities have been violated. Conversely, if the set is taken away with no procedure at all, the irreducible requirements of institutional justice can still be satisfied by a hearing on whether to give it back to you. If it turns out you are entitled to the set, you will have been inconvenienced by not having it during the proceedings. But so the other side would have been inconvenienced if you had kept it and it had turned out to be theirs. Inconvenience is the price of living with other people. Granted, as much as possible the inconvenience ought to fall on the party that wants to set the machinery in motion (*potior est conditio defendentis*) but it does not all have to.

In a case like this, a philosophical analysis between different kinds of justice is useless. Rather, the competing demands must be weighed and a solution reached that gives a maximum accommodation, and as much of all kinds of justice as can be had. With the problem in this form, there cannot be a single right solution to it. Some solutions are better than others; some are so bad as to be out of consideration, but a number of equally good ones could probably be found. As in other cases where different values and interests militate against one another, an exercise of discretion is called for from those who have to make the choice.

INSTITUTIONAL DISCRETION

Much of our institutional learning is devoted to channeling, directing, and limiting the discretion of those who have decisions to make. I have tried to show in a number of places that a mechanistic approach that leaves no room for discretion makes nonsense of law. On the other hand, a discretion that is not subject to fixed forms and limits makes it no law at all. So the discretion that needs to be exercised is divided into parcels and distributed among the different institutions that make up a legal system. The limits are sometimes provided by rules and principles (for instance those delineating the powers of an administrative agency or the jurisdiction of a court), sometimes by the exigencies of the situation (the power of the President to wage war, or of a policeman to break up a street corner brawl), sometimes by the common consent of the community (the powers, such as they are, of the British monarch).

The institutions that exercise the broadest discretion in a typical legal system are the national and local legislatures. These bodies are charged with making general expectations specific, with reconciling divergent expectations (balancing interests), with orchestrating the rest of the institutional structure, the powers of officials and agencies, the jurisdiction of courts. In some systems, such as our own, all legislatures are subject to limits laid down in the documents — constitutions, charters, enabling acts — that established them; in other systems such as the British, the highest legislature is regarded as omnicompetent.

Traditional theory has it that legislatures constitute one of three coordinate branches of government, the other two being the judicial and the executive branches. The legislative branch is supposed to make laws, the judicial to apply them to particular cases, and the executive to carry them out, i.e., administer social controls in their support. By the doctrine of separation of powers any person or institution belonging to one of these branches is to refrain as far as possible from exercising functions proper to the others. Sophisticated applications of the doctrine leave room for the exercise of "quasi-legislative" and "quasi-judicial" powers by administrative agencies, although these are considered part of the executive branch, and for "interstitial" lawmaking by the judiciary in cases not covered by existing law.

This threefold division of powers is useful in sorting out government functions, but I think there is a tendency to make too much of it philosophically. The important distinctions are technical, not theoretical. The legislator has to work out clarifications and compromises and fit them into dispositive language. The judge has to ascertain specific facts and measure them against general principles or general rules. The executive or administrator has to work closely with individuals and get them to implement community purposes. The skills, the personnel, and the organization required for these tasks differ a good deal, but the institutions do not differ all that much in their place in the overall legal enterprise.

The mistake I find in most separation of powers thinking lies in its sharp differentiation between making laws and doing other things with them. This is another form of a view I took issue with in an earlier chapter: the view that discretion is the same as arbitrary choice. Since the making of laws is largely a matter of discretion, while other operations involve limited discretion or none at all, to equate discretion with arbitrariness is to say that the lawmaking function, unlike all others in the legal enterprise, can be carried out arbitrarily. But as I see discretion, it is not arbitrary at all. It is a knowledgeable and rational response to the practical and moral exigencies of the situation, and to the expectations of the community. A person or institution charged with exercising discretion may instead act arbitrarily, but so may a person or institution charged with applying rules. Public officials are kept within their allotted spheres in the first instance by their own consciences, failing that, by the intervention of other public officials, and, in the end, by what the community will put up with. It might be suggested that a community will put up with more arbitrariness from a legislature than from a court, but I doubt if the evidence will bear out the suggestion. Consider whether your favorite arbitrary statute is more firmly established in the community today than your favorite arbitrary judicial decision. Or, if you prefer, consider whether the people of the free states were more docile to the Fugitive Slave Act than they were to the *Dred Scott* case.

Note also, that while a legislature has a broad discretion, exercising discretion is not all that it does. It too has rules, principles, and analogies to apply. Some of them limit its powers: freedom of speech, for instance, a written constitutional limitation on American legislatures, an unwritten customary limitation on the British Parliament. Others call for the enactment of legislation: an obvious example is the maxim *ubi jus ibi remedium*, referred to above. Granted, I would not go so far as to hold with the medieval theorists that human laws are but specifications of a *natural law* written by God with normative force in men's hearts. There is give and take in the process, and certainly a legislature is expected to respond to political considerations that would not be expected to sway a court or even an administrative agency. Still, there is a great deal in the legislative process that calls for judging a situation in the light of prevailing expectations and personal insights into what is right or wrong: a great deal, that is, that corresponds to the judicial process. There are many cases in which lawyers argue for or against the enactment of legislation in much the same way they would argue for or against a particular decision of a court.

Perhaps the best way of putting it is that the different parts of the legal enterprise, if they are working as they should, will all move together to meet with increasing sensitivity the expectations of the community, and to enunciate with increasing refinement the expectations of the government. As the process goes on, exercises of discretion will tend to give way to principles, principles to rules, but at every level there will be a good deal of all three. It is true in a sense that the legislative branch makes new laws while the other branches give effect to old ones, but it is also true in a sense that the legislature, like the other branches, gives effect to something that was already there.

The legislature is not the only branch that comes up with something new. We are pretty well accustomed to the idea of judicial legislation, but that is only a variant of what I have in mind. It is a peculiarity of the Anglo-American system that a decision of an appellate court immediately becomes a precedent for the decision of future cases (a course of decisions may have that effect in the Continental systems, but not one decision by itself). When Anglo-American judges start worrying more about what kind of precedent they are making than how they are disposing of the case before them, we say they are legislating. We may approve or disapprove of their doing so (most often we are ambivalent about it), but we have no doubt that they are legislating. In laying down generalizations for future application, they are playing the functional part of legislators.

Even when they are playing their own functional part and merely deciding cases, judges must often look beyond the precedents and stattutes of the written law to the same things legislators consider. Take for instance the question that comes before the federal courts from time to time whether a person guilty of occasional lapses from premarital chastity possesses the "good moral character" required by statute to become an American citizen. The judges' decision is based on the standards they think are prevalent in the community. This seems fair enough, since the question is not whether the applicant is wholly commendable, but whether he is good enough to be accepted as one of our number. Judges have not been willing either to follow their own standards instead of those of the community, or to establish community standards by scientific evidence, such as public opinion polls, instead of their own intuitive judgments. In each case, they make a personal judgment informed by a general familiarity with the life of the community, which is what I have characterized as an exercise of discretion. A legislator, considering whether to add an express requirement of "chaste life" to that of "good moral character," would do just about the same.

There is, to be sure, one major difference between judicial and legislative discretion: I have already alluded to it. Despite Mr. Dooley's observation that "the Supreme Court follows the election returns," we expect our legislators to be more sensitive to political considerations than we expect our judges to be. Generally, if I tell my local legislator that if he votes for a certain bill I will endeavor to see that he is not reelected, I will not be acting improperly, nor will he if he takes my threat into account. But if I tell my local judge, who may well be running on the same ballot, that I will try to have him defeated if he votes for the plaintiff in a particular case, I will be acting improperly, and so will he if he is influenced by what I say. Similarly, a legislator who refrains from enacting a law because it will antagonize powerful forces in society is sometimes (not always, but sometimes) doing the right thing. A judge who refrains from a particular decision for the same reason seems necessarily to be doing wrong.

It is not as easy as we might think to see why this should be the case. It is not simply because the judge ought to be following the law uninfluenced by extraneous considerations. It will be as true in a discretionary case like the naturalization one just discussed as it will be in a case governed by specific rules. It is not because the legislator represents the people and the judge does not. To the extent that the constitution is based on popular sovereignty, the judge represents the people as much as the legislature does. And even if no one represents the people — say the legislature is a military junta and the courts are left over from a previous regime — the difference will still obtain. I think it is a matter not of the scope of the discretion committed to the respective branches but of the different considerations governing its exercise.

A judge's primary mandate is to do justice to the people presently litigating before him; a legislator's is to maximize justice in the community. Politics concerns the legislator more than the judge because it is an affair of people in the aggregate, not one of individuals. The desires of major constituencies concern the legislator in the way those of individual litigants concern the judge. The realities of power in the community concern the legislator in the way the idiosyncrasies of the parties concern the judge. The judge's concern in looking at the community is not so much to bring about a more just social order as it is to position the individual litigant justly within the social order as it stands. In doing this, he may bring about profound changes in the social order, but they are, or should be, a byproduct.

Perhaps I can illustrate this conception of the judge's function with an instance in which the judiciary departed from it, with what seem to me unfortunate results. It was a year after the Supreme Court held school segregation unconstitutional that they finally decided what to do about it. They came up with their famous "deliberate speed" order, calling on school administrators to adopt plans under judicial supervision for the overall integration of their systems. They were to take into account the administrative difficulties — reassigning personnel and facilities, redrawing district boundaries, etc. — and overcome them as quickly as possible. The court would have acted more in accord with the judicial function if they had simply ordered particular black students admitted there and then to particular white schools, and left the administrative problems to be coped with as they arose. This is what they did with interstate buses, labor unions, parks, and universities. Looking back, I suspect they would have spared the country a good deal of grief over the ensuing decade if they had done it with schools as well.

People whose functions are executive stand halfway between legislators and judges in the way they exercise discretion. Like judges, they have a responsibility for dealing justly with individuals, and like legislators, they are expected to do the best they can for overall justice in the community. Naturally, the relation between the two mandates can be puzzling. There are, to be sure, cases where one clearly takes precedence. In case of imminent invasion, for instance, most people would think it reasonable to round up suspected fifth columnists and saboteurs to be kept safe until the emergency was over; if an innocent person was picked up in the net, the inconvenience would be his contribution to the common cause. On the other hand, no one (well, almost no one) is for rounding up all the suspicious-looking characters on the streets in order to prevent muggings. But between these extreme cases is a lot of debatable ground. How do we feel about shooting cattle suspected of having anthrax? Putting people out of their homes to build a highway? Being extra lenient on an automobile safety inspection because the owner is poor and needs the car to get to work? Decisions like this require a sophisticated exercise of discretion on the part of the executive personnel making them.

No agency exercises more day-to-day discretion of this kind than do the police. Policemen, like prosecutors, have to decide which criminals to spend the available time and resources on bringing to book. In addition, there are all manner of people disrupting or threatening the tranquillity of the community whom policemen have to decide whether to bring into the criminal process, or to cope with in some other way. A policeman can arrest a traffic offender, give him a ticket, or let him off with a warning. If he sees a drunk on the street, he can look the other way, he can arrest him and prosecute him for public drunkenness, he can arrest him and let him go the next morning when he is sober, or he can escort him home and tell his family to put him to bed. If he catches a boy shoplifting he can start juvenile delinquency proceedings, or he can report him to his parents and let them handle it. If he sees an unruly crowd, he can arrest some of them, he can warn them to quiet down, or he can send for colleagues with clubs and tear gas.

Some of these alternatives are not dealt with by the law; others, if the law is taken literally, are contrary to it. For instance, the process of arrest is supposed to be a means of making sure an accused will be available to answer charges. Arresting a man without intending to prefer charges against him, as in the case of the drunk taken in for the night, would seem therefore to be illegal. But there are cases in which it is the most sensible, and the most humane, thing to do. It is a better way to deal with drunks than leaving them on the street to be robbed or run over. It is probably a better way to deal with political demonstrators than gassing them or breaking their heads — which in many cases would not be illegal. Similarly, if a policeman sees two boys squared off in an alley with knives, he can legally take their knives to use as evidence in a subsequent prosecution, but he cannot legally take them simply to keep the owners from cutting each other up. Often he will do so anyway. There is a case I recall from the British papers a few years ago where the police got word that two teen-age gangs were about to fight. The customary manner of fighting of these gangs was by kicking and stamping with reinforced-toed boots. Accordingly, the police waited at the railroad station and confiscated the shoelaces of any teenager who showed up wearing boots of this kind. Entirely illegal as far as I can see, but there is something to be said for it as against the legal alternative of wading in with tear gas, fire hoses and rubber bullets after the fight starts.

Whether the policeman is morally right to depart from or violate the law in cases like this raises the same kind of questions as are raised when we ask whether other people do right to violate the law. These I have dealt with in another chapter. More to the present purpose is the question of how much scope the community should allow him for doing such things. For my own part, I think the point of encounter between the citizen and the police is a particularly important one for the application of human subtleties that cannot be encompassed in a rule book: it is no place to discourage improvisation.

But police discretion, like any other discretion, must be rooted in an intimate knowledge of the ongoing life that is to be regulated: it is this depth of knowledge that distinguishes an exercise of discretion from a mere arbitrary choice. It seems that a great deal of current feeling that there should be more rigid controls on the police reflects a growing alienation between the police and the rest of the community, especially those parts of the community with which the police most often deal. This alienation has been partly attributed to the fact that policemen generally patrol in cars, so they have no ordinary contact with the people among whom they work. Another consideration is the fact that much police work involves dealing with racial and cultural minorities to which few policemen belong. Putting the police under rigorous legal restraints is a poor substitute for having policemen sensitively in touch with the people they serve, but if we cannot recruit that kind of policemen, there is little alternative.

The citizen's other main contact with executive discretion is through administrative agencies. From a modest beginning with the medieval sheriffs, churchwardens and Justices of the Peace, these agencies have proliferated with the growth of industrial society until now they are involved in almost every aspect of life. You get your driver's license from one. You buy food that has been inspected by another in a store that has been licensed by a third. There is one through which you will seek compensation if you are injured on the job, another that tells you what union you must join, still another that determines how much you must be paid. There is an agency that will give you unemployment compensation if you are laid off your job, another that will give you welfare when the unemployment compensation runs out, a third that will give you social security when you retire. These agencies exercise legislative and judicial powers in the areas assigned them, sometimes making general rules about what people are supposed to do, sometimes determining whether this or that person has done what he is supposed to. At times, they will take a middle ground between legislation and adjudication, negotiating with people over solutions to particular problems. For example, the Securities and Exchange Commission will make regulations about what people must put in a prospectus when they are selling stock, will adjudicate whether your prospectus complies with the regulations, and will tell you what to put in your next prospectus to keep them from troubling you further.

In all these activities, agencies are entrusted with a great deal of discretion, some more than others. The knowledge on which their exercise of discretion is supposed to be founded is called expertise. It is supposed to extend to whatever it is they have been given to regulate: in the case of the Securities and Exchange Commission, securities and their marketing; in the case of an Alcoholic Beverages Commission, the sociology and economics of drinking; in the case of a School Board, schools. The scope of this expertise is taken into account by legislatures in establishing agencies and defining their powers, and by courts in determining the validity of what they do, or exercising judicial review over them. They are generally provided by the legislature with *standards* in the form either of policies to implement or of considerations to bear in mind. It was once felt, and by a few courts is still felt, that failure to make these standards clear enough will result in a violation of a constitutionally-demanded separation of powers: applying standards laid down by the legislature is an executive function, but making new standards is legislative. Most experts in administrative law now feel that this distinction is too naïve, that all we can expect of the legislature is to set reasonable limits to administrative discretion, and that the reasonableness of a particular set of limits depends on the economic, social, and political context in which it appears.

The crucial distinction to my mind is this: The ground for legislative discretion is an overall understanding of community life, whereas the ground for administrative discretion is expertise, an in-depth understanding of a particular aspect of that life. On this basis, we think it appropriate to impose a fairly detailed set of standards on, say, the agency that regulates labor-management relations, while, say, the agency that regulates use of the county airport may need no standards at all. The point is that most of the problems of running an airport — how to trace lost baggage, where to park taxicabs, in what order planes line up for takeoff, where not to smoke — can be solved by a sufficient understanding of what you are about, whereas there are crucial problems of labor-management relations — secondary boycotts, closed shop contracts, dual unionism, etc. — that no amount of expertise can solve. Getting planes in and out, and people to and from planes is pretty much the same process in any community, whatever its social and historical background, or whatever its political or economic system. But how you structure the collective bargaining process and how you relate the individual workman to it depend on what kind of society you have and what kind you want to have.

INSTITUTIONAL TECHNOLOGY

It has become customary in our political rhetoric to ask why, if we are able to land men on the moon, we cannot come up with a just ordering of our own society. It is easy enough to give the question a short answer. Everyone agrees on which way the moon is and what constitutes being landed there, but there is a good deal of disagreement about what constitutes a just ordering of society: One where everyone has a job, or one where everyone can change his job if he finds a better one? One where the press is free, or one where it is required to be socially responsible? Furthermore, even if we knew what kind of society we wanted, pursuing it with the kind of split-second organization required for the moon landings would leave us little opportunity to enjoy it. So much, one might say, for that question. But behind the question one can discern a perplexity that seems to deserve a better answer than the question does. There are in our society undoubted injustices, apparent, pervasive, and identified. Can it be anything other than a failure of heart or will that leads us to put up with them? Surely (here is where the men-on-the-moon part comes in) a society as advanced as ours cannot lack the technical skill to abolish them.

Alas, it can and does. Deploying the resources of a sophisticated legal enterprise to cope with all the injustices invented by a rich and imaginative society requires a good deal of training and experience to do even creditably, let alone with total success. Whether it is done creditably in our own society is not for those of us responsible for doing it to say. In any event, total success is not to be looked for.

A threshold problem in evaluating the technical skill with which our institutions are constructed and operated in the pursuit of justice is presented by our slippery understanding of the justice being pursued. When we speak of justice, or deplore the lack of it, we may mean (a) a moral virtue which leads people to render to others what is due them, (b) a state of affairs in which people customarily do what that virtue requires of them, or (c) a state of affairs in which lapses from that virtue are suitably redressed. The problem occurs when people calling on the President, Congress, the courts, the Federal Trade Commission to bring about justice in the second or third sense, use the tone of moral censoriousness that belongs to an exhortation to practice justice in the first sense.

Since justice is a moral virtue, the failure to render justice is blameworthy. The failure to make my landlord fix my front steps is a failure to render justice.

Ergo, the failure to make my landlord fix my front steps is blameworthy.

Using reasoning like this, a person who will cheerfully junk a three-hundred-dollar used car because it is not worth the cost of repairing will be outraged at having to drop a fifty-dollar damage claim because it is not worth the cost of collecting. It is quite possible that redress, justice in sense (c), is too expensive, and should be cheaper. But it cannot, any more than auto repairs, be obtained without time and effort which someone will have to pay for.

Furthermore, redress, like pills, has side effects. Suppose, for instance, a man seduces a girl under a promise of marriage, and then refuses to marry her. Even in today's swinging society, it would seem he has done her a serious injustice. But affording her redress might motivate him to go through with the marriage in order to avoid the consequences of a lawsuit: a poor start for a relation that is to embody our modern conceptions of togetherness. This is one of the reasons (the possibility of bringing groundless suits for purposes of blackmail, a consideration of institutional justice, is another) why many jurisdictions have abolished the common-law cause of action for breach of promise to marry.

The side-effects problem is still more acute, if slower in manifesting itself, when we address ourselves to major social evils — i.e., pursue justice in sense (b). Thus, forty years ago, it seemed clear that it was unjust for an employer to pay less than a living wage. So we came up with legislation, minimum wage laws, laws favoring unionization, etc. to see that the worker got his due. It is only now that we are beginning to see the side effect: a growth of technology to replace human labor by cheaper ways of getting the job done. From this comes a new portfolio of problems that we are only beginning to cope with. This does not mean that we made a mistake forty years ago. It is simply part of the ambivalence of history. Today's problems arise from the success, not the failure, of yesterday's solutions. Short of the eschaton, justice, even if pursued to perfection, is not pursued to finality.

There are a good many cases of injustice also where the cure is worse than the disease. Even where no actual institutional injustice is required for reaching a substantively just result, the mere weight of the institutional operation may be more than the resulting justice is worth. Often we hear of people who will pay a disputed bill or an undeserved fine, or let the thief who stole their hi-fi set go free, rather than take the trouble to go to court. We can and should make going to court less trouble than it is, but we can hardly make it no trouble at all.

This kind of trouble is greatly magnified of course when broader social issues are involved. The carloads of documents required to set a freight rate, the number of lawyers who are monopolized by a monopoly case, the miles flown by businessmen and bureaucrats attending conferences on air fares, the coordinators, social workers, and accountants saved from poverty by anti-poverty programs are all proverbial. If this weight of institutional activity is great in our own society, it is far greater in other societies that seem to do better about some of the injustices that are perplexing ours. Here again, improvement is possible, indeed, overdue. We would like to provide more justice with less machinery, just as we would like to improve the rest of the technology by which we live. But even with the best technology in the world, just as we may find that the only answer to air pollution is to use less gasoline, we may find that the only answer to institutional proliferation is to use less justice.

IV

PEOPLE
The Final Cause

7

MAN ALONE

NATURAL LAW

If you flatten a forest to build a hideous motel, or if you break up Chippendale chairs for firewood, you may be wronging yourself, your fellows, your posterity, or your Creator, but you are not wronging the forest, the trees, or the chairs. On the other hand, if you kill an innocent human being, even one so commonplace, so isolated, or so unsavory that no one could possibly miss him, you wrong the victim himself more directly than anyone else. A human being, unlike a tree or a chair, is a *person;* he exists in his own right, and for purposes intrinsic to himself. The personal fulfillment proper to him has certainly a social dimension, but it is not a means to any social purpose, or to anything else for that matter. It is his last or ultimate end.

Since his end is within himself, he can be said to have *rights.* If you divert a thing from its proper purpose, you wrong those whom the proper purpose would have served. It follows that if you divert a person from his proper purpose, you wrong him. For me, and for the philosophical tradition to which I adhere, this principle is the cornerstone of human rights.

The principle is complicated by the social and material dimensions of human fulfillment. Though a person's end is intrinsic, he cannot reach it without relating to other people, nor can he do so without making use of the material amenities of the world. Hence, his rights extend not merely to the freedom of his pursuits, but also to suitable arrangements whereby he can relate to others, and avail himself of a sufficient part of non-human creation to meet his needs. In saying this, I am advisedly deriving rights from needs. Since human beings must both relate to each other and share the limited stock of material resources, I think the recognition one person owes to the intrinsic end of another is not limited to a passive noninterference, but demands at least a modicum of active support in its pursuit.

It is to protect the noninterference and to organize the support which people need and are entitled to from one another that we have legal systems. This is why the human person is the final cause, or the purpose, of the legal order. Law is to serve people. It may seem that I have gone to undue lengths to establish so trivial a thesis, but it is a thesis that does not go unopposed in the world of legal theory. Alternative and baneful doctrines are often put forth with great earnestness and zeal: either the law serves some collectivity, race, nation, class, society, or that it serves some metaphysical order, or that it serves its own internal logic with no extrinsic purpose at all. Some of these views I have touched on in earlier chapters. Some I find wholly unacceptable, while others state intermediate goals that the law may legitimately pursue. But none can provide the ultimate purpose of law. This can only be the individual person, because, of all the law deals with, only the individual person has ultimate worth.

While the end of a person is intrinsic to himself, it is not entirely opaque to his fellows. Although everyone has his own life to live in his own way, people can understand the broad outlines of one another's needs on the basis of their common humanity. While I have no way of knowing whether you like artichokes unless you tell me, I can be pretty sure that cyanide is no better for you than it is for me. It is the same with the moral and spiritual life. Each of us has a realm of experience that is closed to the other, but each of us can discern that some things are suitable or unsuitable for the other because they are suitable or unsuitable for a human being. To put the point in a more traditional form, human nature offers a guide to how people should live and what they require from one another. To this guide every human being has access, both as it applies to himself and as it applies to others, through reflecting on his own experience of being human.

Here again, I am stating a doctrine that is far from universally accepted. The leading school of opponents proceeds from a radical empiricism: human nature can offer no guide to human life because you cannot see, hear, taste, touch, or smell it; for all practical purposes it does not exist. The only thing we can know about the purpose of another human being is what he himself states his purpose to be. It is possible with some ingenuity to construct viable moral and legal theories on this foundation, but I prefer to leave the task to those who think it necessary. The perception of human nature is an intuitive one, so I cannot offer discursive arguments in favor of it, but I think I am in good company in being content with it.

A very different objection is the one presented by certain radical Protestant Christians, led by Jacques Ellul. In their view, human nature exists and can be discerned, but it cannot offer any guide to human life because it has been irretrievably corrupted by the Fall. The theological question raised by this argument is worth an extended treatment, but this is not the place for it. Roughly, my response is that the Fall has not so much destroyed the capacity of human nature to offer a guide, as impaired our capacity to follow the guide it offers. Certainly we have no perfect perception of what is good for us, but we are better able to perceive it than to attain it.

To sum up, the ultimate purpose of the legal enterprise is to protect and support the personal fulfillment of individual persons, and human nature can furnish a guide in determining what does or does not contribute to that fulfillment. Accordingly, human nature is a guide to the purposes law should achieve. Put another way, it provides the teleological content of a legal system. This teleological content provided by human nature is what I have in mind when I use the term natural law.

This term has been used in a number of different senses over the centuries. The uses have in common the recognition of something normative in human nature, but they have varied with the character and status of the inquiries to which the concept has been applied. Not all of these inquiries have been legal. In fact, what seems to be the primary use of the term natural law is in the realm of moral philosophy: there are certain ways we ought to behave, because it is our nature to be happy and fulfilled if we behave in these ways, unhappy and frustrated if we do not. It is generally added that these ways are discoverable, at least in theory, by reason, though the reason of any given person may be inadequate to the task. Thus, for the moral philosopher, the assertion that there is a natural law means that morality is not dependent on categorical imperatives, personal preferences, or even divine revelation, but on shared experiences of what people are like.

The use of natural law in moral philosophy supports a theological doctrine of the primacy of the intellect over the will in God. There was (or is thought to have been) a school of theologians who said that God's commandments represent His arbitrary choice of how we must behave. The only thing wrong with lying, murder, adultery, is that God has forbidden them. In the exercise of His complete freedom of will, He might just as well have commanded them instead; then it would have been right to do them, wrong not to. Against this rather bleak doctrine, those who assert the primacy of God's intellect over His will say that God commands us to behave in certain ways because He knows, even if we do not, that we are the kind of creatures for whom it is good to behave in those ways. Thus, God's commandments are a reiteration of the natural law for those whose intellects are not sufficient to discover it by reason.

The notion of natural law as a "law" of divine origin inherent in mankind has given it a certain vogue in contemporary political doctrine. It has become a vehicle for asserting the superiority of the moral order over the legal order. People will say that you must obey the natural law rather than the law of the state when what they mean is that you must do what is right rather than what is legal. This terminology offends a number of people who insist that even though they do not believe in natural law they are as ready as anyone else to defy the law when it would be immoral to obey it.

The traditional legal uses of the term natural law are derived from the moral use. In scholastic theory, human law, the law we are concerned with in this book, is derived from natural law in the same way administrative regulations are derived from statutes. It draws conclusions where the natural law states principles: natural law says you must bring up your children; human law says you must educate them. It makes specific what the natural law leaves general: natural law says to use what is yours in such a way as not to harm your neighbors; human law says not to drive your car faster than thirty miles per hour down the main street of town.

In the seventeenth century, a rationalist school of natural law doctrine grew up to displace the scholastic school. The rationalists were encouraged by Descartes and his followers to place increased emphasis on the accessibility of natural law to reason, and to define the role of human law as drawing conclusions rather than specifying generalities. They tended to believe that whole legal systems could be derived from pure reason without any historical or sociological input. The most important product of this school was the Code Napoleon. It was actually a good piece of legislation, but later commentators have had a field day showing how much it depended on economic and social presuppositions unrelated to the pure reason its framers supposed they were using.

The scholastics never made the rationalists' mistake of excluding existential circumstances from any part in the framing of law. Hence, their system has proved a good deal more durable than that of the rationalists, as a number of modern theorists have pointed out. The weakness of the scholastics, to my mind, is not in their understanding of what human law is supposed to accomplish, but in their understanding of how it works. Their approach depends on a view of law as rules: do

this, don't do that. Having this view, they can use the term law uni-
vocally of the commandments of God, the moral strictures dictated by
human nature, and the laws of men. I have already shown why I do not
think law can be regarded as a set of rules. It follows that moral principles
and divine commands, though they can influence law, cannot correspond
with it in the way the scholastics have in mind. It is for this reason that I
speak of natural law as a teleological element in the legal enterprise rather
than as the set of rules behind legal rules.

This teleological element is the basis for what seems to me the most
persuasive of the various accounts that have been offered for our traditional freedoms — speech, the press, religion. Law must serve individual
fulfillment, but cannot finally bring it about. Hence, it must on occasion
give way to more effective means, or to the individual's efforts to accomplish for himself what no one else can accomplish for him. Natural law,
then, by setting a goal for the legal enterprise, at the same time sets limits
on its scope.

But it does other things as well. The human purposes with which
natural law is concerned enter into every part of the legal enterprise as
the ultimate ground for interpreting and applying legal dispositions.
I have dealt with the role of discretion in law, and have pointed out that
discretion comes from a participant's understanding of the ongoing life
of the community in which the law operates. Natural law controls and
guides that discretion by relating the human purposes manifested in a
particular community to the more basic purposes which all human beings
share. It is the foundation of a broader discretion, drawn from a participant's understanding of the ongoing life not of one community, but
of mankind.

In what follows, I will try to show the place of this natural law in our
own legal system by taking some rather rudimentary aspects of human
nature, and showing how they have entered into the concrete dispositions of Anglo-American law.

HUMAN WORTH

In 1947, the United States District Court for the Southern District of
California convicted a matron named Elizabeth Ingalls on the charge of
holding one Dora Jones in conditions so abject as to amount to slavery.
The abjection was real enough. Dora received the worst possible food
and housing: at one point, she spent a month sleeping in the family
car. She was allowed no time off, and no visitors. She was not even paid.
The situation was maintained by a certain amount of duress. Dora had

been the mistress of Mrs. Ingalls' first husband, had submitted to an abortion in approximately 1908 and was still afraid Mrs. Ingalls would have her put in jail. Why she thought she would be worse off in jail is hard to see.

Despite all this, there were conceptual obstacles to convicting her employer. The applicable statute was enacted by Congress in 1867, presumably to eradicate the last vestiges of the peculiar institution just put down by the Civil War and the resulting Thirteenth Amendment. It is hard to see any historical continuity between Dora Jones and Uncle Tom, or between Mrs. Ingalls and Ole Massa, or even Simon Legree. The antebellum relation was fundamentally juridical. If it persisted beyond the law that created it, it did so on account of habits and expectations to which the law had given rise. Eliminating those habits and expectations must have been the purpose of the 1867 act.

The judge increased the conceptual difficulty of the case by instructing the jury:

A slave is a person who is wholly subject to the will of another, one who has no freedom of action and whose person and services are wholly under the control of another, and who is in a state of enforced compulsory subjection to another.

In fact, only a fraction of the slaves in the old South were so straitly regimented as to fall within this definition. In short, while Dora lacked the juridical or past juridical condition of Uncle Tom, Uncle Tom was not at all necessarily subjected to the existential suppression Dora underwent. The question is what they had in common that made them both slaves within the meaning of the 1867 act.

It is here that natural law comes in. The Civil War was won, and its results embodied in the statute book, by men who believed that Uncle Tom's condition, however idyllic in particular cases under kindly masters, was unworthy of a human being. Before the law, he was a chattel: often a beloved and well-treated chattel, like a favorite pair of slippers, but still a chattel. It was true enough, as Southern apologists pointed out, that many a Northern mill hand was worse treated by his Abolitionist employer than Ole Massa treated Uncle Tom. This was a serious grievance, and another age produced legislation intended to relieve it, but the 1867 statute was aimed at an institution that treated a man not always badly, but always like a thing.

If the statute is to be interpreted in the light of the particular aspect of human teleology it is meant to serve, there is a good deal of sense in applying it to Dora Jones. It is precisely the chattel quality of Dora's lot that seems to distinguish her from other mistreated workers. As we have seen, existing for purposes intrinsic to himself is what distinguishes a person from a thing, and Dora's treatment leaves no loophole where such a purpose can be recognized. There are all kinds of possibilities for hard and coerced service in our society (say you stay on as an ulcer-ridden account executive because your employer threatens to tell your wife where you were on a certain weekend), but none quite like this. In the social environment of 1947, it was harder to treat a person as a thing than it was in 1867, but Mrs. Ingalls succeeded in doing it.

United States v. *Ingalls* is of course not a typical case. But the principle it illustrates, that of interpreting legal dispositions in the light of human worth, is at work all the time. It appears, for instance, in the gradual development of a line of workmen's compensation cases that holds that a person is still at work when he goes into the alley for a smoke, stops to render assistance at the scene of an accident, or even takes a swing at a fellow worker who annoys him. Sometimes the application is subtle. I concur, for instance, in the judicial intuition that a policeman shows insufficient regard for the dignity of a human being when he secures evidence by pumping out his stomach, but not when he secures evidence by taking blood samples from his arm — but it is difficult to give an explanation for my feeling. Other applications, though, are clear enough — like the rule that says you cannot protect your watermelon patch by rigging spring guns to shoot intruders. Human life is more important than property.

Doctrines like this are the beginning, not the end, of analysis. For instance, if human life is more important than property, we have to ask why it is generally held that you can shoot an armed robber rather than give him your property, whereas you cannot shoot a thief rather than let him make off with it. I suspect it is because you are defending your freedom from coercion as well as your property. Or why must you run away from an assailant on the street rather than shoot him, whereas in your own house you may stand your ground? Your house involves both your identity and your sense of security more intimately than other property does; our ancestors considered it a specially heinous offense to attack someone at home. But to illustrate the development of natural law principles more fully let me turn to a different aspect of human worth, man's superiority over brute creation, and show how it has supported a kind of rear guard action against the technological society over the past century.

From earliest times into the nineteenth century, when a combination of sophistication and capitalism brought other ideas to the fore, a chattel that brought about the death of a human being — the cart he fell from, the horse that threw him, the flower pot that fell on his head, the knife his enemy stabbed him with, or the, one he stabbed himself with — was forfeit to the king's almoner for distribution to the poor. It was a *deodand*, or thing to be given to God. The forefeiture was no kind of compensation to the deceased, though it might be given to his family if they were poor, nor was it a punishment of the carelessness of the owner. A chattel belonging to the deceased himself was just as liable to forefeiture as any other. Coke says the chattel is given up "for the appeasing of God's wrath." The eighteenth century commentators attribute the whole doctrine to superstition and perhaps popery. Pollock and Maitland are saying the same thing, though less censoriously, when they find a "sacral element" behind the law of deodands, but they end up saying

Also, it is hard for us to acquit ancient law of that unreasoning instinct that impels the civilised man to kick, or consign to eternal perdition, the chair over which he has stumbled.

As a believer in natural law, I cannot treat unreasoning instincts as cavalierly as Pollock and Maitland do. My view is that if anything is deeply enough rooted in human nature there must be a reason for it: not everything unreasoning is unreasonable. Anyone who takes the Old Testament seriously has not far to look for the source of his sense of outrage when things or animals turn against people. Such a state of affairs was not meant to be: it is a consequence of the Fall, a primordial catastrophe that has made nature intractable to man. We cannot ask our legal institutions to repeal this sentence, but we can seek in them some sign that the ultimate mastery of the situation remains in a just Creator rather than in his rebellious creatures. Handing over the *bane*, the thing that has killed a man, for religious purposes was, I suspect, intended as such a sign.

It is harder to find such intentions as this in modern law, but I think there is something of the kind behind our general feeling that if dangerous articles or processes are introduced into our lives some human being should take responsibility for them. In the course of the present century, this feeling has produced great modifications in our traditional patterns of legal liability. Through workmen's compensation legislation, we have put the responsibility for industrial injuries on those who run the industries involved. Through judicial decisions expanding the duty of care and the warranty of quality, we have made the manufacturer of a defective product liable in most cases to anyone injured by it. Through other expansions of the concept of negligence — attractive nuisance, *res ipsa loquitur*, etc. — we have made the custodians of our industrial technology generally liable for the harm that is done on their premises or by their processes. By another line of cases (most of the early ones involved dynamite), we have established that where a process is so dangerous that it can hurt people without any negligence at all, those who set it in motion are liable as insurers for the harm it does. In the realm of automobile accidents, we have allowed juries to discern negligence in the most trivial forms of inattention, and we are in the process of adopting legislation that will make every car owner buy insurance covering anyone injured by his car, regardless of fault.

To be sure, it is customary to attribute all this expanded liability to nothing more romantic than a growing concern with social insurance. But this explanation overlooks the tenuousness of our actual commitment to social insurance in general: there is little sentiment for extending to all injured persons the protection we now afford those injured by particular processes. It also overlooks the rhetoric we use in expanding liability. The judicial opinions supporting workmen's compensation rest not on insurance but on responsibility:

In excluding the question of fault as a cause of injury, the act in effect disregards the proximate cause and looks to one more remote — the primary cause, as it may be deemed — and that is, the employment itself. For this, both parties are responsible, since they voluntarily engage in it as coadventurers, with personal injury to the employee as a probable and foreseen result.

The expansions of tort liability, by the same token, continue to use the language of wrongdoing in cases where no responsible moralist would try to fix moral fault. It seems that in these cases the wrong is not in doing the injury, but in doing it without accepting responsibility for it. The alternative to imposing responsibility is to say that a vast and often dangerous technology may come upon us with the impersonality of a natural force. To say this is to say that the intractibility of matter is subject to no ultimate control.

It is worth noting, though, that this insight was slow in establishing itself in our law. The misplaced optimism of the nineteenth century stood in the way. If technology is inherently good, a progressive movement by which the sentence of the Fall is to be overcome, a sign in its own right of a just order in the world, the problem of taking responsibility for it does not arise. If it does a person harm, it is probably his own fault, or else he is one of those whom the evolution of the race has destined not to survive. It was a generation that held this view that finally abolished the law of deodands (1846), and developed the fellow-servant doctrine that protected the builders of railroads from the necessity of paying for injuries to their employees. Conversely, it was a generation that had nightmares about people being enslaved by robots that began developing expanded bases of liability.

Today, we seem to be on the verge of a comparable evolution in our ideas about social organizations. Until quite recently – at least until after the Second World War – it was a prevailing view that organizations are inherently good, or at least neutral (i.e., good or bad according to the uses to which they are put). Some people saw it as evidence of progress that we were getting better and better organized, and more capably planned. Those who were unhappy about the growth of General Motors were pleased about the growth of the Federal Trade Commission, or the United Auto Workers, or both. And vice versa. Not until the 1960s did we develop a broad base of sentiment that an organization might be bad or at least dangerous simply as such, regardless of what it was trying to accomplish. This attitude puts the organization on the same footing as the machine. It is here to stay and we can hardly do without it; but our dignity as human beings demands that it not be permitted to jeopardize our well-being without someone taking responsibility for it.

The legal authorities of recent decades are ambiguous on this kind of responsibility, just as those of the late nineteenth century were on responsibility for machines. However, the good authorities offer a basis for development along the lines I have in mind. To illustrate, let us look at two cases, a good one from 1949, and a bad one from 1933. The good one, *Ewing* v. *Black,* involved a salesman named Robert Black of Nashville, whose employer had deducted Social Security contributions from his pay for six years, but had failed to pay the money over to the government. Black needed credit for those six years in order to get full benefits when he turned 65 and retired. The Social Security people said that they had no record of his making any contributions during those years, and that they were very sorry but the time provided by statute for correcting their records had expired. They admitted there was no way Black could have found out his contributions were not being recorded, but felt it was just one of those things. The court felt otherwise. Black having done exactly what he was supposed to do to collect full benefits, was entitled to collect them.

Note how much the stand taken by the government in this case resembles the stand taken by a nineteenth-century railroad when someone got run over by a train. It is unfortunate, but no one is to blame, and nothing can be done about it. The wheels of federal administration, like the wheels of commerce, must continue to roll on their appointed and fundamentally beneficent course despite the occasional flattening of someone who gets in the way. The court's decision reflects the more humane view that progress does not require people to put up with being run over.

The bad case is *Solow* v. *General Motors Truck Co.* Solow worked for the company under the supervision of a man named Holmes, who fired him, and, "actuated by express malice," according to the court, entered a notation in the personnel records to the effect that Solow had been let go because of "Communistic attitudes" that made him impossible to work with. Some months later, he was planning to go into business on his own, with borrowed money. His intended lender contacted his former employer as part of a credit check. The employer had a clerk of unblemished innocence named Quinn, who copied the notation from the record just as the malicious Holmes had entered it, and thereby spoiled Solow's business deal. Solow sued for libel.

The rule in libel cases is that a response to an inquiry of this kind enjoys a qualified privilege. That is, since you passed out the information for a good purpose, you cannot be guilty of a libel unless you were actuated by express malice, as Holmes was. General Motors argued that Holmes may have had the requisite malice, but it, the company, did not. The rule on this point is that an employer is liable for what his employee does in the scope of his employment but not otherwise. The United States Court of Appeals for the Second Circuit, speaking through Chase, J. (usually a better judge than that), found that there was no basis within these rules for attributing malice to General Motors in making the statement about Solow. Holmes, the malicious one, had authority to fill out records, but not to answer inquiries, whereas Quinn, who answered the inquiry, had no malice. To be sure, Holmes must have known that the record he made up would be used for answering inquiries: to that extent, he was responsible for the libelous answer Quinn gave. But since he was not hired to take responsibility for answering inquiries, his responsibility was not imputable to General Motors.

This means General Motors, through the division of labor, can seriously violate people's rights without being liable for doing so. The problem is that by traditional master-and-servant learning a master cannot be liable unless some specific servant does something which (a) renders him, the servant, liable, and (b) was authorized by the master. This approach will not do when the wrong is committed not by a specific servant but by a clutch of them following standard procedures. What is needed here is a new doctrine making the master liable not for the wrong committed by an individual servant but for that committed by the organization. We have authority for this in the blasting cases, to which I have just referred. If an industrial process is so constituted that it can be free from negligence and still harm people, then whoever introduces that process into the community is responsible for the harm it does. By the same token, if an organization is so constituted that it can be free from malice and still grind out libels, then whoever turns that organization loose on the community should be responsible for the libels.

The growth of computer technology in the past decade has made this approach increasingly persuasive. The computer has all the dangers of the organization, and most of those of the machine as well. It will not break arms and legs unless it is used to run a machine, but it can break reputations, job opportunities, and credit ratings simply by doing its primary work of data storage and retrieval. Theoretically, it can print out misinformation through mechanical failure, or through someone pressing the wrong button: the same kind of thing that goes wrong with machinery. More often, what happens is that the programmer makes a mistake, or the wrong data is fed in in the first place: organizational failings like that involved in the *Solow* case. In any event, the scale of the possible misinformation, and the difficulty of correcting it are new. We are hearing more and more stories about someone who finds that erroneous or irrelevant facts about him have been stored in one computer, then passed on to other computers all over the country without further human intervention. When he tries to find the error and correct it, the only replies he gets are from more computers. Lawmakers have tried to deal with this problem by giving the citizen a right to see the data that has been assembled about him, and to tell some human being if it is wrong. I do not think this approach goes far enough. Following the analogy of the blasting cases, I would make anyone who disseminates data assembled by other people an insurer of its accuracy, and of the legitimacy of disseminating it.

This discussion is intended not so much to offer a solution to the problems of technology, badly as we need one, as to show how a principle like human worth can enter into the bread-and-butter dispositions of a legal system. *United States* v. *Ingalls* involves a question of statutory interpretation. My proposed liability for the use of computers involves the application of precedent. In both cases, it is our understanding of the value and purposes of human beings that delineates the scope of the legal dispositions we have to work with, and the basis for extending them to new situations. The rationality of the legal enterprise lies in its effort to respond to the enduring necessities of human nature. And in that rationality lies its capacity for orderly development to keep pace with life.

HUMAN FREEDOM

The purpose of a man's existence is a problem both to him and to others. It is uniquely his own, yet subject to the necessities of common human nature. It is rooted in his own interiority, but it requires him to relate to others. To discern and follow it, he must pose a series of questions, and find the answers as best he can. We, his community and government, recognize the freedom to which he is entitled in this pursuit, sometimes because we have no answers to give him, sometimes because for one reason or another we think his answer will serve the exigencies of the case better than ours. Of course, if we really have no answer, his freedom will raise no difficulties, since we will have no occasion to interfere with it, and he in turn will have no occasion to claim it at our hands. A genuine agnostic will not interfere with other people's religion, a person who knows nothing about the stock market will not interfere with their investment decisions, and a stranger to their community's affairs will not interfere with their vote.

The serious questions about freedom are those that arise when we have an answer and must worry about whether to impose it on others or not. I want to stress this point because there has been a tendency in our thinking, or at least in our rhetoric, to treat our commitment to freedom as a product of intellectual, moral, or religious neutrality. People say, for instance, that we adhere to religious freedom because religion is a private matter on which we do not wish to take a stand as a community, or that we adhere to freedom of speech because we expect good ideas to prevail in competition with bad ones. There are cases where we actually do believe things like that, but these cases are not the ones where anyone talks about freedom. That is, we are prepared to admit that free discussion will give us the best decision on where to put the new firehouse. For that very reason, everyone is content to let everyone else have his say. I let you talk not because I believe in free speech but because I think what you have to say may be worth listening to. The cases where the commitment of our society to free speech is really tested involve people who by the prevailing consensus in the community are not worth listening to at all — anarchists, white supremacists, single tax men — people with ideas that we are sure could never make their way in the intellectual marketplace, and that we would not embrace even if they did. It is the same with religious questions. No one worries about his freedom to hold any view he pleases on a question like the manner of Christ's presence in the Eucharist, because we think this is not a question on which the community should take a collective stand. The kind of people who have to claim religious freedom are the ones who believe that God has commanded polygamy or forbidden blood transfusions: things which by the prevailing consensus of our community He has not done.

I see three main types of cases in which our own legal system prefers freedom over the imposition of official or generally accepted answers. The most philosophically compelling is the one where the individual will have no benefit from an answer unless it is his own. Religion furnishes a clear example. Nothing would please me more than to have everyone embrace what I understand to be the true religion. But since that religion is concerned almost exclusively with personal commitment, there is nothing much I could do, even if I had the power, to bring about that state of affairs through law. Similarly, the government's computers might be able to choose a better wife for a man than he could find for himself, but unless he was willing to have her, she would hardly make him happy. Or, whatever benefit someone derives from living in beautiful surroundings will probably be lost if he considers them ugly, even if they conform to the soundest canons of taste the community affords.

Next, there is a class of cases in which it is felt that a person is generally in a position to make a better decision than anyone else could make for him. You are apt to know better than anyone does, for instance, whether Dr. A understands your particular ailments better than Dr. B. For this reason, people who propose legislation for government health care try to arrange for as much scope as possible in choosing your physician. Corporate managers are apt to understand the corporate business better than judges; hence, courts generally do not interfere with management decisions unless there is evidence of bad faith. The same principle is followed in cases involving emergencies. X comes after you with a knife. Do you really have to shoot him to save your life? You are walking along a highway during the rush hour. In the prevailing traffic pattern, are you safer on the right even though the general rule says walk to the left? Should the doctor perform a Caesarean section, or should he allow labor to continue a few hours longer? On matters like this, any decision within the realm of rationality and good faith will be respected, even if those reviewing it would have decided differently.

Finally, there are cases where the authority to decide seems, for good or ill, to reside in the individual rather than the community. I see freedom of speech as falling into this class: it is every person's business to decide what ideas he will accept and communicate to his fellows. The freedom of a parent to decide how his child will be educated is in this class also. Besides specific freedoms like these, there is a more general right of a human being to make his own decisions about his own affairs. Here it is more the quantity than the quality of interference that must concern us. It is quite possible for a series of restraints, each legitimate in itself, to add up to a pattern of regimentation inconsistent with the dignity of a human being. This danger to freedom is not as well countered in our legal system as some others are, though some of the legal restraints on administrative action probably have something of the kind in view. The main barrier to overall regimentation is political; whether it is sufficient remains to be seen.

Difficult legal problems concerning the scope of freedom come up when someone wants to do something that runs afoul of an extraneous policy pursued by the law, or interferes with the enjoyment of mainstream amenities by other people. An example of the first type is the member of a snake-handling cult: a form of religious expression we are generally willing to suppress. Having decided that God has not commanded people to handle poisonous snakes, we do not impose that theological position on those who reject it, but we allow the general public policy against snake handling to apply to members of the cult as it does to anyone else. This result is rooted in the basis for recognizing religious freedom in the first place. We are not interested in having anyone abandon this doctrinal error unless he does it freely, but we can stop him from getting bitten by snakes if we stop him handling them, whether freely or under compulsion. Of course, suppressing the central rite of his religion may do him more harm than the snakebite. This makes for a further complication of the problem, which I have taken up in another work.

An example of the second type is presented by the Amish parent who does not want to send his child to high school. Both his freedom of religion and his freedom to educate his child in his own way argue for letting him do as he chooses. The child's right to be educated in the ways of the mainstream argues the other way. Our Supreme Court decided recently in favor of the parents. I suspect it is some lack of confidence in the mainstream life-style that led them to do so; it is the same lack of confidence that leads me to applaud their decision. One who believed strongly enough in what the schools were teaching would probably find it consistent with his commitment to freedom to take a harder line.

When we weigh the freedom of the deviant against the desirability of implementing accepted standards across the board, we take the motive behind the deviation fairly heavily into account. We give the least scope to a person whose deviation is merely bizarre; we give only a little more to one whose deviation is philosophically motivated. The religiously motivated deviant fares better than the philosophically motivated (witness the conscientious-objector cases and statutes), but worse, oddly enough, than the one who departs from accepted standards for purely practical reasons. Take, for instance, a law requiring a parent to provide necessary medical treatment for his children. Suppose a man has violated this by refusing to get eyeglasses for his nearsighted son:

1. He will be least apt to get in trouble if his reason is that he has

bought a bottle of pills from a quack doctor and believes that they will cure his son's myopia.

2. If he takes his son to a faith healer and relies on the power of prayer instead of eyeglasses to make his son see clearly, it is about an even bet whether the courts will interfere with him or not.

3. If he feels it is the duty of every public-spirited citizen to boycott the manufacturers of eyeglasses because of the outrageous prices they charge, he may get a few words of praise from the courts, but they will not let him off.

4. If he thinks boys with glasses look like sissies, no judge will give him the time of day.

This hierarchy of motives is not quite what one might have expected, but it seems to make a certain amount of sense. It is quite likely that our society has not enough tolerance for the merely bizarre: the ease with which harmless eccentrics can be committed to mental institutions and kept there under our law is scandalous, and they experience a good deal of harassment even when they are loose. Still, man is a rational animal, and it seems appropriate to value reasoned dissent more highly than caprice. Giving religion a preference over philosophy has been attacked on the ground that it violates the constitutional prohibition against establishing a religion. The courts have met the objection by broadening the concept of religion to include commitments that do not necessarily depend on a belief in God. Religion thus broadly understood seems entitled to its place ahead of philosophy. The truths or supposed truths on which one founds one's life are seldom held at the level of mere intellectual conviction. They go much deeper, and interference with what they require cuts correspondingly deeper into one's humanity.

Why, then, is action based on this kind of commitment less protected than action based on practical judgments about day to day affairs? Perhaps the point is that the capacity for practical judgment, being farther removed from the core of one's personality, is in more danger of erosion than the capacity for religious commitment, and, at the same time, in less danger of falling prey to self-deception. If a person needs his religion more than he needs his foolishness or gullibility, it is also true that he can do more harm with it, both to himself and to others. Conversely, a state that sets out to put down foolishness and gullibility will probably do even more harm than one that sets out to put down eccentric forms of religion.

Of course, human freedom is a fact as well as a claim. We have to cope with it as a fact even where we do not accept it as a claim. Suppose, for instance, a publisher claims he is free to put out dirty books, and we tell him that freedom of the press does not extend that far. He is still free to put out the books because we have no very effective way of stopping him. In this sense, people are also free to desert their families, poison themselves, rob, rape, and murder. The law has to deal with this kind of freedom first by encouraging people not to exercise it, and second by picking up the pieces when they do.

As to encouragement, I have already referred to the work of the law in maintaining an ambiance conducive to moral behavior. There are also cases in which it recognizes and implements specific rights to moral support. For instance, it is because we believe a citizen is entitled to moral support from his government, that we allow the defense of entrapment in criminal law. The police are not to seek out people likely to succumb to temptation, supply the temptation, then prosecute them when they succumb. There are also private rights to moral support, as in the marriage relation. I find instructive on this point an old (1927) New Jersey case called *Pike* v. *Pike*. The case involved a man who married an actress of somewhat dubious reputation, and concealed the marriage for fear of losing financial support from his parents. While the wife was living as a single woman in a New York hotel, she fell into adultery, and the husband sought a divorce on this ground. The court held that knowing of her weakness, and depriving her of the moral protection that would have gone with the social status of a wife, he had so far contributed to her behavior that he could not complain of it. In these days of no-fault divorces, we may quarrel with the result of the case, but the point that a husband is bound to provide a modicum of moral support for his wife seems well taken. It can be applied to other matrimonial offenses besides adultery: say a man by indifference drives his wife to drink, then seeks to divorce her because she is an alcoholic.

Here is another line of cases that involves rather similar principles. A man is injured by a tort or an industrial injury, then commits suicide because he cannot stand the pain. Can his widow sue the tortfeasor for wrongful death or the employer for workmen's compensation? If he is so mentally deranged by his injury as not to be responsible for killing himself, the answer is clearly yes. In my opinion, the answer should be the same even if the suicide appears to be a morally responsible act. Even if he has sinned in taking his own life, the injury, by subjecting him to temptations the ordinary person does not undergo, should be regarded in law as a cause of what he has done. Some courts follow this view fairly explicitly; others reach the same result by going out of their way to find mental derangement. Many courts, though, will allow no recovery unless the suicide's mental condition was such as to preclude all vestiges of moral responsibility. Their approach seems based on a kind of Bible Belt freewill theology by which a sin can have no cause beyond

the evil disposition of the sinner. My own view accords with a more traditional theology which recognizes the responsibility of the sinner, but
also recognizes the part played in his fall by the people and circumstances
that tempt him or fail to support him.

The subject of compensating the widows of suicides brings us to the
work of the law in salvaging situations brought about by the moral failings of those involved. I pointed out earlier that this kind of salvage has
come in many areas, divorce for instance, to replace simpler concepts
of enforcing specific rights and redressing specific wrongs. As a way of
dealing with people who have done something wrong, it seems in accord
with the Christian traditions of our society. It is gaining a place as a sup-
plement to punishment in our treatment of criminals: witness our efforts,
such as they are, to get prisoners back into society when they have served
their terms. It has affected our conception of the right of privacy so that
a person is entitled to live down old scandals and complain if anyone gratuitously brings them back to light. It has led the courts to take a new
look at the problems of illegitimate children and unmarried couples —
to grant welfare benefits to unmarried mothers and their children, to
give workmen's compensation benefits to a woman for the death of the
man who has been supporting her, to straighten out property tangles
when a liaison breaks up. These judicial and legislative initiatives are not
without difficulties, but for the most part their tendency is to give a more
humane stance to our legal system.

INTEGRITY AND OPENNESS

So far, we have considered freedom as a limitation on the powers of
government, and as a problem the legal enterprise faces in trying to accomplish its goals. But ultimately, freedom is a positive commitment of our
society, a goal in its own right. It is something every human being requires if he is to relate to God and neighbor, and so become what he is
meant to be. This positive understanding of freedom is reflected in a
number of distinctions we make in applying traditional constitutional
principles. For instance, we extend to commercial advertising a great deal
less constitutional protection than we do to other forms of speech and
writing. Restricting the way a man sells his product does not bruise his
spirit in the same way as restricting the way he communicates what
is on his mind. For the same reason, the courts in obscenity cases try
(not always very successfully) to distinguish between hack pornography
and honest communication about sex.

Man's capacity to relate to God and neighbor often requires protection, as well as forbearance, from the law. This protection has both personal and social dimensions. The social dimensions, which I will take up in the next chapter, include support for the family and community structures in which relations between people are realized, and amelioration of the conditions of poverty and dependency that sap creative choice. The personal dimensions, our immediate concern, involve two main interests, privacy and emotional security.

Your power to control the intimacy with which others enter into your person and affairs depends on your right to privacy. Without it, you would have great difficulty relating to others: it would be meaningless to admit them to intimacy, since you would have no power to exclude them. Friendship, like hospitality, is a matter of opening doors, which you cannot do unless you have them to open.

Your emotional security is your feeling (as opposed to your intellectual conviction or your faith) that you live in a world that is willing to have you live in it: a world that offers reasonable possibilities for loving and being loved. Without some measure of this kind of security you would not have the courage to get up every morning and face the rest of the world.

In our system, the right of privacy extends to both person and affairs, to the former more fully than to the latter. It is theoretically a tort to touch or threaten to touch another person in any way without consent — or at least a social context in which consent may be presumed: kissing a girl when you take her home from a date, tapping a stranger on the shoulder when he has dropped something, giving artificial respiration to an unconscious person. Breaking in on a person's physical privacy without actually touching him may also be a tort. A doctor, for instance, who brought a curious friend to watch him deliver a baby was held liable to the mother on this ground.

The depth of the intimacy in question has a good deal to do with the scope of the protection afforded. This is why rape has always been taken so seriously. A man who rapes a woman is punished more severely than a man who knocks out a couple of her front teeth, even though he may have done her no physical harm at all. Control over one's sexuality is more important than control over one's teeth. To be sure, the rapist may often do great psychological harm; nevertheless, it is control, not psychological well-being, that is protected by the law. Thus, it is no defense to a rape charge (though it may raise problems of proof) that the victim is a prostitute, that she has consented to the same man on another occasion, or that generally she values her sexual favors lightly. In one case, a man was convicted of attempted rape although the victim had just offered to have intercourse with him for ten cents.

Some invasions of the person are so gross, or so dehumanizing, that they will not be tolerated even if consented to. For instance, a man who burned his initials with a cigarette on the insides of his girl's thighs was held guilty of a crime although she was willing. So was a man who hired a prostitute to submit to a whipping. The hiring seems to make matters worse. Even normal sex tends to be severely treated if it is sufficiently commercialized. Making a cash transaction out of what ought to be a personal relation is more destructive of the human personality than is a disordered or trivialized pursuit of personal relations. Worse, if anything is capable of being bought, the poor will be strongly tempted to sell it. This is probably why recruiting and organizing prostitutes is taken more seriously than prostitution itself, or why the squalid living and working conditions of many migrant farm workers are objected to even though they have consented to them. The perception that the degradation of poverty is made worse if everything is subject to purchase and sale has been slow in coming. Time was when a dentist would transplant healthy teeth from a poor man willing to sell them into a rich man willing to buy. Today, he would probably lose his license for doing such a thing.

Privacy in one's affairs is a fuzzier notion than privacy in one's person. It has had so much treatment in the legal literature that there is not much point in trying to delineate its exact scope here. The term right to privacy was first used in a famous article published in 1890 by Warren and Brandeis. They argued that this right provided the actual principle underlying a number of decisions that had customarily been classified in other ways. Their view has gradually gained acceptance. It has been applied to such matters as a creditor complaining of his debtor's defaults by posting a large sign in his store window, and a landlord rigging an electronic listening device in his tenants' bedroom. Lately, the Supreme Court has used it (somewhat disingenuously in my opinion) to prevent states from interfering with contraception and abortion. At one point, it was also widely used in redressing gratuitous publicity. There are now some freedom-of-the-press decisions that leave that aspect of it in doubt. In any event, the general idea seems established.

Protection against emotional distress presents a good deal more of a technical problem for the law than does protection against invasion of one's person or affairs. Obviously, any normal person encounters in the course of his life a good deal that jars him emotionally, much of which he would be spared if other people behaved with more sensitivity and good will. Our machinery of justice has neither the resources nor the sophistication to afford everyone a remedy against whoever tactlessly or even maliciously wounds his feelings. Accordingly, our courts have felt the need to set limits. As matters stand now, they will allow mental distress as an element of damages when you are complaining of some other kind of wrong: e.g., slander, assault, alienation of affections. They allow recovery where the mental distress has been caused by sufficiently outrageous conduct (for instance, a woman collected damages from the estate of a man who cut his throat in her kitchen) or a pattern of harassment (bill collectors are sued fairly often under this head). Where the defendant's conduct was egregiously insensitive, rather than malicious, there may still be recovery if the mental distress results in physical harm, as where a woman suffered a miscarriage when her husband was brought home covered with blood after an accident. A case that people keep bringing, but usually lose on, is that of a mother who suffers from shock when someone negligently runs over her child. The upshot of all the cases is that emotional security is now recognized as a legally protected interest, albeit one that requires a certain circumspection in the enforcement.

All this may look a little remote from the positive aspect of freedom with which I began this discussion, but I think it is not. A free man is not merely one who can go where he pleases, speak his mind with impunity, or thumb his nose at his leaders without going to jail. In the last analysis, a free man is one who has no need to be timid in receiving others, or fragmented in giving himself. Even in a free country this kind of freedom is hard to come by and easy to lose. It is as a Christian, not as a citizen, that I hope to achieve and maintain it. But to a certain limited extent the forces working against me are set in motion by the malice or obtuseness of other people. To that extent, the law can play an important part in helping me to be free.

8

MAN AND HIS NEIGHBORS

It is hard to put fundamental legal principles into a social context, because the context keeps changing. Whether the world is moving toward some final consummation, moving in cycles, or just moving, it is not, and never has been, standing still. Society, however, for all its metamorphoses, serves human needs that are fairly constant. While the world endures, people will probably go on needing to work together, to eat, drink, and be merry together; to love, embrace, confront, or impress one another; to open their hearts and minds to one another; to offer one another what consolation they can in the face of illness, privation, anxiety, and approaching death. Orchestrating the efforts of individuals and groups to meet these needs is a work of the legal enterprise; hence, the needs themselves are an important part of the teleology of law. Like the more personal teleological elements we took up in the last chapter, they guide both community and government in the development of new legal dispositions and the application of old ones.

MAN AND MAN

The first thing people need from each other is simply to be recognized as people: the recognition Martin Buber has in mind with his famous distinction between the *I-Thou* and the *I-It* relations. I am to recognize you, and try to relate to you, as *Thou*, a being with an interiority analogous to my own, rather than as *It*, a datum, a convenience, or perhaps an obstacle in my solipsistic pursuits. We have seen in passing some of the things the law can do to encourage one kind of relation instead of the other. It should probably be doing them more advertently than it is. I think our most serious failing in this regard is our lack of attention to the quality of human relations within the legal enterprise itself. The experience of being an *It* before the law and its ministers furnishes a pervasive theme for both the literature and the sociology of alienation in our time.

It was something the folk wisdom of our ancestors guarded against. In old proceedings, those involved, whatever befell them, were always present as sentient fellow-beings to the people disposing of their affairs. One is often impressed with the personal, almost conversational, quality of the colloquies accompanying even the most brutal or bizarre applications of the law. It would seem that an eighteenth-century criminal was more present as a human being to the people who came to see him hanged than a modern criminal is to the people who come to see him rehabilitated.

The traditional wisdom is still reflected in rules like the one requiring the presence of the accused in court at every stage of a criminal proceeding. If he has a good lawyer, much of what is done could be done just as well without him, but it is good for everyone involved to keep remembering that it is a real person with a real face whose life or liberty is being disposed of. Those who value the institution of the jury tend to raise the same kind of consideration:

Our civilization has decided, and very justly decided, that determining the guilt or innocence of men is too important to be trusted to trained men. If it wishes for light upon that awful matter, it asks men who know no more law than I do, but who can feel the things I felt in the jury box.

The idea behind such rules and institutions as these is that people understand each others' affairs not through expertise but through connaturality: I know what people are like not because I have studied them, but because I am one of them.

Paradoxically, the increasing humanity of the substantive law in modern times seems to have had a great deal to do with the erosion of connatural elements in its application. We have drawn more and more on economic, sociological, and psychological insights to reform our law, and on experts to give those insights their full scope. Decisions affecting the quality of life are continually being made on the basis of data that ordinary citizens cannot understand. To those who make decisions of this kind, the rules of administrative law with their insistence on personal confrontation (notice and hearing) of those affected, are experienced as irrelevancies and obstacles in the implementation of their beneficent expertise. Recent controversies over the participation of the poor in efforts to eliminate poverty furnish one of many examples of this process at work.

The classic example in administrative law is that of the institutional decision. Is the requirement of a hearing satisfied if the person who hears you does no more than put down what you say and feed it, along with other information, to the upper-rank administrators who actually decide your case? In 1915, the House of Lords, in *Local Government Board* v. *Arlidge,* answered the question in favor of the organization: a hearing does not necessarily mean a hearing by the person who is to make the decision. The Supreme Court of the United States took the opposite view of the famous *Morgan* litigation (1936), though how far they have adhered to it since is problematical.

The situation presented by these cases is in fact a puzzling one. Entitling everyone to a full hearing at a top level of administration will paralyze the processes of government by taking up high officials' time with matters of interest only to the parties. On the other hand, bestowing broad powers of decision at the lowest level will decentralize the policy-making function to the point of incoherence, and expose people to arbitrary decisions by a swarm of petty officials. The usual compromise is to give the lower-echelon administrator, who sees people face to face, power to apply general principles and policies laid down by his superiors, and then to empower someone further up the line to review his proceedings without hearing the case over again. If all this is done well, it will probably suffice to avoid both impersonality and arbitrariness; unfortunately it is often done badly.

The need for efficiency, like the need for expertise, makes for impersonal application of the law. A judge can get through his cases faster without a jury than with one, and a computer can come up with answers quicker than a judge can. With jury dockets five or six years behind in some places, many people feel they are getting more connaturality than they can afford. A number of expedients have been mooted, some even tried: turning personal injury cases over to panels of arbitrators, or putting testimony on video tape, editing out all the objectionable parts, then playing the remainder to the jury while the judge does something else. Above all, attorneys are constantly settling cases by applying rules of thumb in negotiation with one another. I get advertisements every so often from a company that has computerized this whole process, and will tell me on the basis of my responses to a questionnaire about a case exactly how much I should settle it for. All this is ingenious, and perhaps necessary, but it is a far cry from the ideal of presenting a personal claim face to face to someone with power to decide it.

Our criminal processes impose comparable pressures with far more baneful results. Here especially, it is our very humanity that has made us less humane. The procedures we have developed to protect people accused of crime are so sophisticated that a man can be in and out of court a dozen times listening to motions he does not understand before he is heard or hears his accusers on the merits of his case. Meanwhile, the overworked and underpaid lawyers for both prosecution and defense are doing just what the personal injury lawyers do, and trying to settle the case. In the end, a man accused, say of rape, who insists he never saw the girl, will find his own lawyer urging him to split the difference and admit he beat her up, but did not rape her.

In addition to appearing inefficient and ill-informed, connatural decision-making has often been seen as arbitrary. If you are judging on personal intuitions and general experience of life, who is to say you are not judging by mere whim? From this misgiving comes the agitation for "strict construction" by the courts, and more definite standards to guide administrative agencies. Similar considerations have led judges and legal scholars, notably Jerome Frank, who was both, to urge that the civil jury should be abolished, or at least made to render a *special verdict* showing what it has found to be the facts of the case, instead of a *general verdict* showing only who wins.

It is the same quest for standards that produces all the forms we have to fill out and read nowadays. People with discretionary decisions to make — college admissions officers, personnel managers, foundations — use the forms to pin down their criteria; then, as often as not they pore over them looking for some human consideration that their formulated criteria have been inadequate to encompass. The dilemma is a real one: the conflict between arbitrariness and impersonality has no final resolution this side of the eschaton.

I think we can find a modus vivendi, though, if we generally recognize that a human being has as much right to confront those who make decisions about his affairs as he has to confront those who accuse him of a crime. Judgment, like accusation, is a primordial human relation. It is as personal as sex, and produces the same sense of violation if it is impersonally done.

Given this recognition, the competing values — expertise, efficiency, objectivity — can be accommodated one way or another. The high-level policy decisions can be expressed in general rules and principles, to be applied by lower echelons to individual cases. Or the upper echelons can correct specific errors in the original proceedings, as our appellate courts do, rather than address themselves at large to the merits of the case. A range of other devices is available in particular situations. Preserving a human presence in a sophisticated, efficient, and even-handed legal system is not easy, but it can be done.

MAN AND WOMAN

The crucial personal relation for most people is that of love between a man and a woman. The role of law in supporting this relation is obscured by a nomenclature that is more concerned with "the family" and "sex" than with love. Actually, the law does a number of things to help the course of true love run smoothly.

These days we think it runs smoothly if lovers marry each other and live happily ever after. This was not always the case. Medieval people tended to see love as an exotic and extramarital ideal, and to overlook its affinities for the theology of Christian marriage. The work of domestication took several centuries.

The traditional objection to marrying for love is that it is imprudent. One is apt to fall in love with a bad provider or a bad cook. Misgivings of this kind are often reinforced by family and community pressures based on social and dynastic considerations, or even on brute cash. Also, many theorists of the subject have suggested the converse of this objection: if love is bad for domesticity, domesticity is worse for love. The sentiment is so fragile that even the prospect of a few decades of P.T.A. meetings and taking out the garbage is enough to kill it.

In the face of these objections, the law made a number of false starts before it settled in its present pattern of encouraging the love match. Medieval law was largely on the side of venality. For instance, a guardian could offer a marriage to his ward, and if the ward refused, the guardian could sue the ward for the profit he planned to make on the deal. The only concession, one extracted from King John at Runnymede, was that the proposed spouse had to be of the ward's social class. Rules of illegitimacy, elopement, forced marriages, and breach of contract to marry were along the same economic and dynastic lines.

By the end of the seventeenth-century, though, the courts had decided that a third person should not make money out of a marriage. The House of Lords decided in 1695 that a marriage broker cannot sue for a fee: "Marriages ought to be procured and promoted by the Mediation of Friends and Relations and not of Hirelings." Soon after came rules against compensation for parents. In more recent times, we have widened still further the gulf between marriage and business by deciding that someone who talks an engaged person out of marrying is not subject to the same liabilities as outsiders who interfere with other contracts. Indeed, by now most people seem to feel that a contract to marry should not be enforced at all: it is inappropriate to make anyone pay damages for not marrying.

Two cases which helped define a personal conception of marriage seem worth special mention. One, *Merrill* v. *Peaslee,* decided in Massachusetts in 1888, involved a man who had committed a "matrimonial offense" that justified his wife's leaving him. Contrite, he besought her to return. She wanted a financial consideration to do so, and he complied by giving a note to a trustee in her behalf. *Held,* the trustee cannot enforce the note. If she is to return, forgiveness, not money, must be the motive. About a generation previously, Elizabeth Barrett Browning had written, "If thou must love me, let it be for nought except for love's sake only." Holmes, J., dissented.

The other case is *Perez* v. *Lippold,* decided in 1948, early in Mr. Justice Traynor's distinguished career on the California Supreme Court. It declared the state's miscegenation law unconstitutional. This was six years before the federal school segregation decision. "Separate but equal" was still the general rule, but Traynor, speaking for a majority of the court, held that there can be no separate but equal matrimonial opportunities. The individual of your choice is unique and irreplaceable. "Human beings are bereft of worth and dignity by a doctrine that would make them as interchangeable as trains." So much for Magna Carta and its concern for marriage within your class.

As for the theorists' objection that love cannot survive the vicissitudes of married life, it is not true. Love is not eroded by domesticity, it is eroded by time. Marriage, whatever its sociological vexations, is in essence a bid to transcend this mutability, by

> The awful daring of a moment's surrender
> Which an age of prudence can never retract

to put love beyond the reach of waning powers, encroaching triviality, personal inconstancy, and discouragement:

> By this, and this only, we have existed
> Which is not to be found in our obituaries
> Or in memories draped by the beneficent spider
> Or under seals broken by the lean solicitor
> In our empty rooms. . . .

Fidelity to their own beginnings is perhaps the best tribute the middle aged can pay to the ideals of the young.

The need and desire to give beyond recall and be faithful to the gift is to my mind the primary justification for the legal institution of marriage. Law supports — for some, it constitutes — the irrevocability of the gift. In my theology, marriage is an ontological union: if there is a law holding it together, that law is not the state's. Still, I am grateful to the state for such encouragement as it gives. For others, with different beliefs, the state actually constitutes the union. It is not simply that the law imposes obligations and makes divorce somewhat difficult. It is that by making an official profession of their relationship lovers become committed to it.

At this point, the theorist raises a final paradox. Is not commitment itself the negation of love? Love is a free gift, and how can one make a free gift of what he has already given beyond recall? Andreas Capellanus in his vast twelfth-century ideology of dalliance, the *De Amore*, makes the point this way in what purports to be a rescript of the Countess of Champagne in response to a couple seeking enlightenment:

We declare and we hold as firmly established that love cannot exert its powers betweeen two people who are married to each other. For lovers give each other everything freely, under no compulsion of necessity, but married people are in duty bound to give in to each other's desires and deny themselves to each other in nothing. Besides, how does it increase a husband's honor if after the manner of lovers he enjoys the embraces of his wife, since the worth of character of neither can be increased thereby, and they seem to have nothing more than they already had a right to?

What is wrong with this formulation is its naïve conception of rights and duties. It presupposes that one cannot act freely in fulfillment of a duty, or receive something freely to which he has a right. In the moral realm, this is nonsense. If you believe in free will, you believe that a person who does right does it freely, because he could have done wrong. If you believe in determinism, you believe no one does anything freely. On neither theory can it be said that you do wrong freely but right under compulsion. For the believer in free will, the faithful spouse acts as freely as the extramarital lover; for the determinist, both are equally unfree. Fidelity to the original undertaking, then, is as much a free gift, as much a gift of love, as the original undertaking was.

The legal issue is more complicated. I have defined a legal right as something the government expects the community to recognize and the community expects the government to enforce. If the obligations of marriage were not enforced at all, it would be hard to say that it was a legal institution, or that it gave anyone legal rights; on the other hand, if they were enforced vigorously enough, it might indeed be said that the spouses could not love one another because they were not free. By accepting an ideology that puts love and marriage together, the law commits itself to a middle course.

On the one hand, it does not allow much in the way of direct coercion. There is a dictum of the great Lord Mansfield that a husband has a right to seize his wife wherever he finds her, but in 1891 E. H. Jackson, who, with the help of a solicitor's clerk, stuffed his wife into a carriage as she was emerging from church with her sister, was forced to give her up on a writ of habeas corpus. More recently, there was Mrs. Nanda, who was ordered by a court to stop hanging around and disrupting the domestic felicity of her husband and a Miss Atkinson, with whom he was living. Litigants are duller on this side of the Atlantic, but I have no doubt the law is the same.

On the other hand, the courts do pass on the rights and duties of spouses. In most states, the grant of a divorce or a separate maintenance order will depend on a showing that one or the other of them has done something wrong. The relevant forms of misconduct, mental cruelty, desertion, adultery and the rest, are carefully analyzed and classified in the literature and the reports. Even where there is no-fault divorce, some kind of failure must be shown to satisfy the requirement of an "irretrievable breakdown of the marriage."

Third persons are expected to respect a marriage even more than the parties are. There is a tendency these days to abolish the traditional suits for criminal conversation (i.e., adultery with the plaintiff's wife) and alienation of affections. However, there are still many places where a paramour or an officious in-law will be subjected to a substantial judgment, or occasionally to an injunction. Meanwhile, there is an increasing tendency to allow one spouse to recover damages for physical injuries to the other based on loss of *consortium*, the totality of comforts, sexual and otherwise, that one might expect from a healthy husband or wife.

There is no point in continuing this sketch of the law of domestic relations. My purpose with it is simply to establish that the commitment married people have to one another is not so coercively enforced as to prevent their adhering to it freely if they adhere at all, and yet that it gives rise to sufficient expectations to be regarded as a source of rights. The law, like other institutions of Western society, has undergone a long evolution in its attitude toward the personal relation between man and woman, but it has now settled on support for those who keep the personal and juridical relations together and marry for love.

MAN AND SOCIETY

While relations between one human being and another are the fundamental ones in people's lives, the ones the law is most conspicuously concerned with are those between a person and *society*. This term has hard usage these days, but seems to have no official definition. For our purposes, we can take it as designating the whole matrix of relations one person can have with others. How people fit into this matrix will determine in very great part how they find friendship, recognition, help, and whatever else they need to live together as human beings.

Society is meant to serve human needs. To the extent that it does so, it renders people what is due them, and therefore is just. But the needs in question can be met in more ways than one. It follows that justice, as such, offers no comprehensive blueprint for society. Thus, the pursuit of justice by the legal enterprise takes for its starting point the existing structures of society, whatever they are. To this extent, people are right to see the law as an appendage of the status quo. Also, to the extent that a just ordering of society is less vulnerable to overthrow than an unjust, the pursuit of justice itself casts the law in a conservative role. Still, the legal enterprise is not intrinsically committed to any particular organization of society, whether the status quo or some other. It is a part of the ongoing life of the society in which it operates, and embraces both static and dynamic elements, as the rest of society does. If it works well, it will direct whatever elements it finds toward the provision of those things every society owes its members.

First among these, I suppose, are the bare necessities of life: food, shelter, and clothing. As soon as men began driving animals so other men could spear them, or dwelling under roof beams that took more than one person to raise, they required some kind of society to provide these necessities. Concomitantly, they required some kind of law to determine how the people who killed the animal were to divide the flesh and the skin, or which of the people who built the house were to live in it. From beginnings like this, the division of labor has gone farther and farther, bringing with it laws about wages, pensions, prices, land use, allocation of resources, unemployment, consumer protection. Politicians, political theorists, and economists are continually concerning themselves with matters of this kind, and calling on the legal enterprise to give effect to their concerns.

Society defines work, as well as organizing it. It determines whether your particular contribution is one it will pay for, like tea tasting, or one it will not, like bird watching. There is nothing but social convention to say that a man who rides a horse around a race track is earning his living, whereas a man who rides a horse in pursuit of a fox is being idle. Society also has a good deal to do with determining whether what you earn is a living. The fact that an American slum dweller eats better, dresses better, or has more gadgets than a rich Eskimo, a nineteenth-century farmer, or a medieval squire does not console him if he lacks the wherewithal for what his own society regards as a fully human existence.

In our age of cheap transportation, this relativity of standards gives rise to a difficult problem for lawmakers. A migrant worker can come into a high-consumption society like ours, work under conditions abject to the point of inhumanity by our standards, but not all that bad by his own, and save up enough money to live in what passes for modest comfort when he returns home. The question is whether he should be allowed to do this: Should an affluent society arrange immigration and employment controls to keep out people who are willing to work under conditions unacceptable to the locals? There have been debates along these lines about Mexican farm workers in the United States, Portuguese waiters in England, Italian factory workers in Germany. There is a comparable debate from the opposite direction about whether Malawi should permit her citizens to be recruited for work in South African mines.

For a poor country, tourism presents a similar problem. Facilities that keep the locals fairly happy will not do for a rich American or European on a holiday. Should the local authorities permit foreigners and those who cater to them to buy land at prices farmers cannot compete with; erect luxury hotels and golf courses that citizens cannot afford to use; and hire waiters, limbo dancers, and chambermaids to work at better wages than they could get rendering serious services for their own people? Many a tropic paradise has wrestled with these questions in the past few years.

For my part, I think the law should restrict these migrations of poor people into rich societies, or rich people into poor ones. Like certain transactions I took up in the last chapter, they seem to me basically ways of selling human dignity for cash. Obviously, if the cash is needed the temptation is strong: the loss of dignity is never as palpable as the material gain. This is why the intervention of law is so important.

Beyond the material necessities of life, society provides more intangible amenities of equal importance to human beings, and of equal interest to legal theory. For most people, for instance, the sense of identity and basic orientation toward life depend on having an accepted place within a defined society. Theoretically, a person could work these matters out for himself, but his hold on them will be tenuous unless he gets some support from his society. The need is one we are apt not to notice except when it is not being met; hence, it is largely minority groups that are bringing it to our attention at the moment. But it was a World War II deserter named Trop who elicited a statement on the point from the United States Supreme Court. They held that depriving him of his citizenship was a cruel and unusual punishment forbidden by the Eighth Amendment:

There may be involved no physical mistreatment, no primitive torture. There is instead the total destruction of the individual's status in organized society. It is a form of punishment more primitive than torture, for it destroys for the individual the political existence that was centuries in the development. . . . In short, the expatriate has lost the right to have rights.

Another amenity is what I call "externalization." A human being has an inescapable need to impose his personality on some part of his external environment: by building or planting, painting or decorating, writing down his thoughts on a piece of paper, or simply taking something in his hand and remarking to himself "this is mine." His appropriation of things and places in this way requires some validation by society to be secure. Our own legal system provides this validation through the two institutions of property and contract. If you own your own home, it is the law of property that makes it yours; if you rent it, you have it under a contract. If you build a house, it carries the impress of your personality through property rights, of the architect's through contract rights. The two institutions between them determine what part of your environment you can express yourself upon, or at least call your own.

The legal institutions are of course not coextensive with the human necessities that called them forth. Legally, for instance, a corporation owns its factory in the same way you own your house, but the moral and philosophical significance of the ownership is very different. The bigger the corporation, the more tenuous is the connection between its legal ownership and the human purposes the institution of property is meant to serve. People have often used philosophical principles of private property to oppose government interference with big business, but their arguments will not stand up.

In fact, any kind of organization tends to militate against the satisfaction of the need for property. Simone Weil gives this example:

The principle of private property is violated where the land is worked by agricultural laborers and farm hands under the orders of an estate manager, and owned by townsmen who receive the profits. For of all those who are connected with that land, there is not one who, in one way or another, is not a stranger to it. It is wasted, not from the point of view of corn production, but from that of the satisfaction of the property need which it could procure.

This is not to say that our society cannot serve human needs without shifting over to an economy of small holdings and workshops. It is heedlessness, not efficiency, that makes us permit the erosion of people's proprietary stake in the economy. To this heedlessness the law has contributed. It was not intended, for instance, that our farm subsidies should operate more to the benefit of large agricultural corporations than to that of the sturdy yeomanry we had in mind. It was not intended that our provisions for allocating taxes between years should encourage big businesses to absorb small ones. It was not intended that our antitrust laws should encourage oil companies to own service stations instead of dealing with private owners. These things came about by accident, because no one was paying attention to the need for personal ownership.

Outside the realm of business, the law has a better record. It is encouraging to find that our real property law charges a land speculator who shuffles papers in an office with notice of what he would have found out if he had looked at the land. It is encouraging to find that if someone wrecks my furniture our tort law will not limit my recovery to the amount the items would have brought on the second-hand market. Other fragments of encouragement are found in cases holding that you are entitled to put things where you please on your own land without being guilty of contributory negligence if your neighbor's negligence sets them on fire, that a woman who has to support her old parents cannot make them leave their own house and move in with her, or generally that people can use their own things in their own way without being subjected to other people's conceptions of either prudence or value. With a little effort, our law could support a broad humanization of proprietorship.

The last, and to my mind the most important, of the intangible amenities a human being needs from society is the chance to accomplish something with his life. He is largely dependent on the social context to tell him what constitutes an accomplishment. A poet could take little satisfaction in a poem that moved only himself, or a scientist in an invention that no one else had occasion to use.

In our society, we tend to fuse the two goals of accomplishment and sustenance. You are rewarded according to the value of your contribution to the economy, and you support yourself and your dependents with the rewards thus assembled. The same reward determines both your accomplishment and your living standard.

This social convention, commonly known as the work ethic, has a certain affinity for the scriptural mandate to eat your bread in the sweat of your face, but our consumption patterns make the affinity a bit tenuous. Most of the consumer goods we come by in the sweat of our faces these days are hard to think of as bread. They are honorific, like mink coats and Cadillacs, labor-saving (sweat-of-your-face-saving?), like washing machines, or frivolous, like electric can openers. There is nothing in nature or revelation to make us value these things, or admire people who earn enough to afford them.

The most serious objection raised against our system is its irrationality. The economic forces that provide so many more of the good things of life to an account executive than to a school teacher do not represent anyone's reasoned judgment about the value of their respective contributions. Nor is there a reasoned decision about priorities behind the fact that we spend more money on tobacco, watches, and jewelry than we do on housing. To my mind, although this objection is well taken in particular instances (among them both the examples I just gave), it is not universally so. To seek a rational overall plan is to push rationality farther than it will go. We can make some rational judgments about the value of social functions, and when we do we should implement them – as the British have done in the case of medical care. But there is no rational basis for assigning priorities between pizzas and comic books, concerts and power lawn mowers, avocados and high-heeled shoes.

Taken as a whole, then, our haphazard arrangements for determining what accomplishments will receive the most fulsome recognition, what contributions the most copious rewards, are simply a part of our culture. I cannot agree either with those who see them as somehow inherent in the nature of things or with those who see them as intrinsically unjust. History has produced them, and history will no doubt replace them one day with something else. But I also disagree with those who say it was inevitable that history should have produced these arrangements rather than other ones, or that it will come up with specific ones in the future. I accept as a matter of faith that history is going somewhere, but neither my observation nor my theology tells me by what route it is to arrive. Meanwhile, with this, as with the rest of life, it is for the legal enterprise to enhance the possiblities for good and reduce those for evil in the situation it encounters here and now.

Let us see what possibilities our present system has to offer. The most important plus value to my mind is that there is a tendency to reward the achievement of results, and so encourage people to approach problems creatively. This is not universally done. In some societies, and in some careers in this society, rewards and recognition are gained by mastering and following approved methodologies (ancient Chinese civil service; medieval European medicine; modern American school administration), or by commending oneself to other people (most ecclesiastical or literary careers in the eighteenth century; most careers in advertising, television production or politics today). Rewarding methodology tends naturally to stifle creativity. If it is widely done, it produces a remarkably stable but somewhat dull society. Also a rather brittle one: the stability can crack very rapidly when new problems come up, witness China, in the late nineteenth century. Rewarding the ability to commend oneself to other people is destructive of personal relations. If your career depends on impressing someone, you inevitably start thinking of him as a problem — an *It* — rather than a fellow being. In comparison a system where it is an accomplishment and a living to build things, grow things, distribute things, learn, teach, cure, or even make money has a good deal to recommend it.

But a system based on results carries the seeds of its own destruction. The most spectacular results are achieved by people who use lots of machinery, and develop simple methodologies for other people to follow. On this fact is founded the system we call capitalism. Theoretically, this term refers to any economic arrangement in which those who furnish capital can expect to be compensated, but most people use it to refer to a general social system in which major accomplishment requires access to an organized following and an accumulation of capital beyond the reach of the ordinary citizen. Thus, the term is most often used pejoratively. Those who approve of the system refer to it as free enterprise. It seems to me, though, that free enterprise and capitalism are not alternative terms for the same thing. Rather, capitalism as we generally experience it tends to be destructive of free enterprise. To the extent that people need a great deal of capital to embark on an enterprise, enterprise is not free.

Against this background, I would like to see the law address itself to a wider distribution of the opportunity to earn one's living by productive, and, if possible, creative accomplishments, preferably in projects of one's choice. We should start worrying about a person who has nothing decent to do as we have long worried about one who has nothing decent to eat. We could modify our tax laws to encourage employment as they now encourage accumulation of capital. In some lines of endeavor, we could modify the conditions of competition to give more scope to individual craftsmen and small businesses. We could modify our industrial technologies to increase job satisfactions. I do not believe the industrial revolution inevitably condemns the lower echelons of the economy to dull and unrewarding work. It is entirely possible to develop complex technologies in which everyone involved has a task worthy of a human being. In our economic system, we will have such technologies if we arrange our tax laws, our labor laws, our licensing laws, to make them profitable.

If we need a radical change it is less in our economic system than in our attitude toward it. We must recognize that the conditions under which it bestows recognitions and rewards are not "natural." Human beings produced them, and human beings can change them to serve human ends. We must also recognize that the things we make and do with our economy do not, for the most part, serve inescapable human needs. Unless making and doing them gives people pleasure or a sense of accomplishment, we can just as well let most of them go. With these principles understood, we can develop just laws about our economy as we do about other things.

STRUCTURAL PRINCIPLES

Theorists discern a number of principles governing the way society ought to be organized. I shall deal with four of these, which affect the work of the legal enterprise in relating the life of society to personal needs.

The Principle of Social Justice. I have indicated that people are entitled to certain things from society. Since justice consists in rendering to everyone his due, we can say that a society is just when it affords these things as far as it can, and unjust when it does not. But insofar as justice is a moral virtue, it or the lack of it can be attributed only to individuals, not to society. A question therefore arises: What kind of moral judgment are we making about individuals when we say that a state of society is just or unjust? To answer that question, theorists have developed a concept called *social justice*. We may define social justice as that virtue which moves me to support as far as I can an ordering of society that will render to everyone his due. It is to be distinguished from *commutative justice*, which moves me to render to everyone what he is entitled to specifically from me (pay my debts, support my children, not wreck my neighbor's house), and from *charity*, which moves me to provide particular people with things they may be entitled to from society, but not from me (say I give a friend money when he is out of a job, or take an orphan in off the street).

A couple of illustrations will help make the distinction clear. Say the prevailing wage for trash collectors in the community is not enough to live on. I practice commutative justice when I pay my own trash collector more than the prevailing wage: the laborer is worthy of his hire, and a worker is entitled to a living wage. I practice charity when I give money to another trash collector who lives down the street. As an individual, he has no just claim on me. If I have a moral duty to relieve the poor, there are a dozen others as poor as he whom I could have chosen instead, and I have not enough money to relieve more than one. I practice social justice when I support a minimum wage law for trash collectors.

If my parents were poor, I would practice commutative justice by sending them money. I practice charity if I send money to relieve the poor of Vietnam or Bangladesh. But I practice social justice when I contribute to the United Fund in my own city, because that is a means adopted by the local community to meet people's needs.

The failure to distinguish between social justice on the one hand and charity and commutative justice on the other gives rise to some unfortunate legal doctrines. The most pernicious and pervasive is the one that treats welfare legislation as a form of charity. Since the person on welfare has done nothing to earn his money, it cannot be commutative justice to pay him. So anyone who has not understood the concept of social justice will attribute the payment to charity. The misconception is neither merely terminological nor merely academic. It has supported invasions of the personal liberties of welfare recipients that would not be tolerated if anyone else were subjected to them.

The classic case on this is *Wilkie* v. *O'Connor* (1941). The facts are more dramatic than usual, but the state of mind was at one time universal, and has not yet died out. Wilkie was an old man who lived under a barn. His old-age pension was cut off by the welfare authorities when they could not persuade him to move into a "suitable home." He appealed to the court, contending he had the same right as anyone else to live where he pleased. The court would not have it:

Appellant also argues that he has a right to live as he pleases while being supported by public charity. One would admire his independence if he were not so dependent. . . .[I]n accepting charity, the appellant has consented to the provisions of the law under which charity is bestowed.

If you substituted social justice for charity in this passage, you would make nonsense of it. It is generally recognized among those who concern themselves with the legal problems of the poor that the beginning of wisdom on the subject is a recognition that our relief arrangements are an attempt to do justice, so that the poor are entitled to what we give them, and cannot be harassed as a condition of receiving it.

There is an older case, *Adams* v. *Tanner* (1917), that illustrates the confusion of social justice with commutative justice. The particular problem the case dealt with has disappeared with the old constitutional restraints on economic regulation, but the confusion is still worth observing. The case involved a statute of the state of Washington forbidding an employment agency to collect money from a person seeking work. There were serious abuses that led to the enactment; also, the proponents of the law felt that since a person had a right to a job it was wrong to make him pay for one. But a majority of the Supreme Court (dissenting opinion by Brandeis, J.) held that finding jobs for people who needed them was a useful trade, and a person engaged in it was entitled to be paid: the law was unconstitutional. The opinions show a curious failure of the majority and the dissent to address one another's arguments. The majority says nothing about the claim that a worker has a right to a job without paying for it; the dissent says little about the claim that one who performs the useful service of finding someone a job has a right to be paid. The problem is that both claims are legitimate. The majority's position rests on a principle of commutative justice, the dissent's on a principle of social justice. The problem for the court, then, should be seen not as determining which of the two claims is ill founded, but as determining how the two kinds of justice relate.

It would seem that if commutative justice inescapably calls for doing one thing and social justice for doing the opposite, it is commutative justice that must prevail. Social justice aims at an ordering of society as a means for ultimately serving individuals, whereas commutative justice serves individuals here and now. To violate commutative justice is bad in itself; to implement social justice is good only with respect to an end. Hence, to implement a demand of social justice at the expense of a demand of commutative justice is to use a bad means to a good end, and therefore is impermissible. But if you implement the demand of commutative justice at the expense of that of social justice, you are tolerating a collateral and remote evil for the sake of a present good, which it is legitimate to do.

This line of reasoning is important in setting the standpoint from which problems are to be considered, but it is not every case that calls it into play. For instance, in the *Adams* case it is possible to do what social justice requires without violating commutative justice. The commutative principle is that if you need a job and I find you one you ought to pay me. This presupposes that I have already found you the job. It does not prove that I am entitled to offer you my services, − the thing the statute wants to stop me from doing. It is society that put me into a position to offer my services, and society can legitimately make me stop. It follows that in the *Adams* case the claim in commutative justice is illusory, and there is no obstacle to implementing the claim in social justice.

The following, on the other hand, is a case where a claim in commutative justice was improperly, indeed, outrageously, to my mind, subordinated to one in social justice. A welfare agency had custody of a child, and placed her in the care of foster parents; a device which has done away in great part with orphanages, and is obviously a better way to take care of children who have no parents able to care for them. Pursuant to the agency's policy, the foster parents agreed when they took the child to hold her subject to the orders of the agency, to surrender her on demand, and not to try to adopt her. After some years of this arrangement, they became attached to the child, and endeavored to persuade her mother to let them adopt her. For this violation of agency policy, the agency revoked the fostering agreement and demanded the child back. When the foster parents refused, the agency brought habeas corpus and won.

The argument for the foster parents was that a child needs a loving family relation, that this child had a family who were willing and able to provide such a relation, that the agency was not able to provide such a relation in any other way (they admitted that they would probably have to institutionalize her if they won), so it would be unjust to the child to take her away – a matter of commutative justice. The agency's argument was that the foster home system is important to the welfare of many children, and its integrity should be maintained against these people who were trying to undermine it – social justice. Here, the foster parents seem to have the better of the case because of the conceptual argument I made above and because the agency's argument is (as arguments based on social justice are apt to be) the more tenuous of the two. The foster home system could survive an unfavorable judgment here better than the child's well-being could survive a judgment for the agency. An attempt to implement social justice always involves a prudential judgment – what ordering of society will best serve human purposes. Prudential judgments of this kind are very apt to be wrong. Other things being equal, you should follow the judgment prevailing in the community, wrong or not, unless you have an alternative to offer. But other things are not equal when there is a specific wrong proposed to someone who is present here and now.

The Principle of Subsidiarity. "Just as it is gravely wrong to take from individuals what they can accomplish by their own initiative and industry and give it to the community, so also it is an injustice and at the same time a grave evil and disturbance of right order to assign to a greater and higher association what lesser and subordinate associations can do." This statement of the principle of subsidiarity comes from Pius XI's Encyclical, *Quadrigesimo Anno*, where it is called a principle "fixed and unshaken in social philosophy." I find it persuasive, though Pius does not offer much argument in support of it, nor does John XXIII, who reiterates it in *Mater et Magistra*. I suppose the reason it makes sense is that following it gives more people more say concerning their own affairs. I have more influence on decisions made in South Bend, Indiana, where I live, than on decisions made in Washington, New York, Los Angeles, Geneva, or Rome. If I pick up the telephone at a venture, I will probably be able to get two or three state legislators, directors of several local companies, and the manager of a local television station, all of whom will listen to what I have to say. If I try my Senators and Congressman, directors of General Motors, DuPont, and Chase Manhattan, and the heads of ABC, NBC, and CBS, I will be hard put to get past any of their secretaries. They are not to blame for this: they could not get their work done if they were as accessible as people with merely local concerns. I will naturally feel more creatively involved, and less powerless, to the extent that my affairs and those of my neighbors are dealt with by local people I can talk to instead of by national and international figures to whom I have no access.

We must note two caveats here before we go on. First, the principle says only that functions should not be performed at a high level when they can be performed just as well at a lower. It does not say that they should be performed at a low level even if they can be performed better at a higher. It offers no support to the advocates of nostalgic inefficiency. Second, the principle deals with the allocation of functions proper to society, i.e., not exclusively reserved to the individual. It is not an excuse for eroding the individual rights I discussed earlier. Participation in other people's control of your affairs, however effective, cannot be a substitute for controlling them yourself when you are entitled to do so.

Subject to these limits, the principle of subsidiarity offers a useful guide to the distribution of social functions. In our politics, it is well accepted. I know of no one who says the national government ought to do things state and local government can do just as well. Even the most ardent advocate of federal power is prepared to accept the burden of showing the inadequacy of local alternatives. In our economic life, the situation is less satisfactory. Some large businesses are effectively decentralized, but there is a tendency to put small businesses together into larger units, and to run the larger units from the center, partly because doing so means that fewer people will have occasion to think — or be thought about.

In a complex society, the applications of the principle are far from clear-cut; certainly, traditional distinctions, federal-state-local in government and big-little in business, will not serve. In the anti-poverty program, for instance, it was generally felt that the federal government had to intervene to exclude state and local government in order to maintain participation by neighborhood representatives. It is highly coercive activity on the part of a federal agency that keeps television networks from crowding out local programming. Large businesses may commit discretion to local managers, while small ones may rigidly follow policies developed by national trade associations. In short, the principle is a guide, not a substitute, for a sophisticated pragmatic approach.

The Principle of Equality. On the pediment of the United States Supreme Court Building is written in large letters "Equal Justice under Law." The aspiration thus enshrined seems to be compounded of three elements. One is a formal legal postulate: treat like cases alike. Another is distributive justice, one of the forms of justice discerned by traditional philosophy. The third is a philosophical or theological principle: all human beings are of the same ultimate worth, or worth in the sight of God.

Treat like cases alike has affinities for Kantian ethics, but as it stands it is exclusively legal. To violate it outside some kind of legal context would be bizarre, but not otherwise objectionable. It is a purely formal postulate because it offers no basis for determining what cases are alike. To make such a determination, we must decide whether the differences are material (that one murderer is sane, another mad) or immaterial (that one has red hair, the other black). This point was dealt with in Chapter One.

Note that it is like cases that we are to treat alike. Differences in people, even if they are otherwise material, are not to be considered unless they are part of the case under consideration. The fact that the landlord beats his wife will not keep him from collecting the rent. As the old learning put it, there must be no respect of persons.

Distributive justice calls for an equal allocation among the members of the community of the benefits and burdens of those projects which the community undertakes. It does not address itself to what projects the community should undertake, or how the benefits and burdens of life in general should be distributed. It is violated if villagers do not have an equal chance to pasture their cows on the village common, or members of the public to send their children to the public schools.

It is violated also if burdens like taxation or military service are unequally distributed. It is often felt that distributive justice also requires giving everyone an equal vote, i.e., an equal voice in determining what the common benefits and burdens shall be. I would accept this if there were only one community with which to reckon. Often, however, the franchise needs to be adjusted to give appropriate weight to subordinate communities in the counsels of larger ones. The medieval governance of countries by estates and cities by guilds is an example: the United States Senate is another. Despite several decisions of the Supreme Court, I see no reason why regional balance in state legislatures should not be a third.

At the moment the geographical definition of communities poses the most difficult problem of distributive justice we have in American law. Is it just to let relatively affluent suburban communities distribute their own benefits and burdens among their own inhabitants without regard to the problems of the inner city? Are the suburbanites unjust when they resist being annexed to the inner city and being made to pay city taxes? Should they be made to accept a fair share of low cost housing in their territory or of disadvantaged children in their schools? Does the state, by allowing a rich community to spend its own tax money running its own schools, discriminate against children who live in a poor community with a lower per capita tax base? All these questions have been litigated in the past few years and will no doubt be litigated further in the future.

Equalizing benefits within a defined community has not troubled us much since it was established that a city cannot maintain parks, swimming pools and libraries exclusively for whites. There is still a question, though, about whether it is necessary or appropriate to make up for past discrimination by giving specially favorable treatment to former victims: a case on this has just gone up to the Supreme Court, and come back without a decision on the merits. Other issues are in the process of being raised. May a state maintain a school system where all instruction is in English when many of its inhabitants speak only Spanish? Must a state that maintains schools for normal children also provide education for deaf, blind or retarded children insofar as they are able to learn?

Equalizing burdens raises problems mainly in the realm of taxes. A tax should be no more burdensome to one citizen than to another. Does this mean that if I pay a dollar you should pay a dollar too (poll taxes and some license taxes work this way) or that we should pay equal percentages of our resources (real estate taxes, sales taxes, and in Indiana the income tax) or should rich people pay a higher percentage than poor people (federal and many state income taxes)? Most economists favor the third alternative, on the theory (they call it marginal utility) that you need your tenth dollar more than you need your millionth, and can part with much of the latter more easily than with a little of the former. The increasing (though by no means universal) tendency to prefer the graduated income tax to other forms of revenue reflects this view.

Until a few years ago, we had another problem of equalizing burdens in assigning draft exemptions. It was widely felt that the student deferment became unjust when the Vietnam war came along and draftees stood a serious chance of being killed. While garrison life in Fort Benning, Georgia may be more burdensome to a person who would otherwise be in college than to one who would otherwise be riveting auto bodies, the prospect of sudden death is as much a burden to one as to the other.

The principle that people are of equal worth is the most important element in our understanding of equality. Perhaps for that very reason, it is the one whose legal consequences are the hardest to pin down. It is directly invoked only to establish the point that you cannot sacrifice the life of an innocent person to save your own: A will kill you if you do not kill B; you are stranded and will starve to death unless you eat C; your boat will sink unless you throw out D. These are all cases appearing in the reports, but they are obviously of peripheral concern. What we really want to know is whether all these conceptions of equality can give us any basis for evaluating the conditions of inequality we see all around us.

I am afraid I have to give this question a fairly involved answer. I have three theses to offer. First, inequalities of condition are purely cultural. They do not and cannot correspond to any philosophical or theological norm outside the culture. Second, considered as a part of the culture, they are not intrinsically unjust: there is no principle of justice that entitles you to something simply because other people have it, and for no other reason. Third, they are often extrinsically unjust: within the particular society that supports them they often lead to unjust results.

The traditional theological support for inequality has been that it is the will of God. By putting you in your particular circumstances, God has called you to a station in life which it is your duty to accept. This proves too much. By the same line of reasoning, a person who was born naked resists the will of God if he puts on clothes. From the fact that everything that happens is God's will, it does not follow that God wills it to go on happening.

A more modern justification that has been offered for inequality is merit. Because you are handsomer, smarter, stronger, more honorable, more abstemious, or more industrious than I, you somehow deserve more copious recognitions and rewards from society than I do. This principle has had a good deal of vogue in recent years. We have even been regaled with the term meritocracy to refer to a society based on inequalities determined by it. I am extremely skeptical. In the first place, we have the Scripture to remind us that the race is not always to the swift nor the battle to the strong, but time and chance in all. Anyone should be very chary of flattering himself that he has reached his exalted position simply by satisfying the ostensible criteria for deserving to be there.

Moreover, the criteria themselves are suspect. The principle that people are of equal worth forbids us to assign unequal conditions based on the relative worth of whole human beings. Hence, we must apply partial criteria, and these will be relevant only in a social context that makes them so. Even if the race were always to the swift, swiftness would bring top distinctions only if society decided to hold a race instead of a chess tournament or a wrestling match. So the idea of merit is illusory: it is really a matter of being born or adopted into a culture that happens to value something you have to offer.

Another ground offered for inequality is need. People with a more complex intellectual or emotional makeup than others need a more complex lifestyle than others, and a greater allocation of resources to support that lifestyle. This reasoning is especially drawn on to support unequal educational opportunities: if everyone is to develop his talents to the full, one with more talents to develop needs more education than one with less.

It seems to me that this criterion also is culturally determined. A talented child does not need an education in the way a paraplegic needs a wheelchair. He needs an education because he lives in a society that offers no career befitting his talents unless he is educated. In other societies, he could develop the same talents by learning to track animals, interpreting sacred books, or building a small shop into a great business, without any major expenditure of economic resources on his training.

John Rawls, in his recent very influential book, offers to justify some inequalities by what looks rather like a common good argument: an arrangement whereby A is better off than other people will be just if and only if the other people are better off than they would be without the arrangement. We need doctors, we cannot get them unless we pay more than the prevailing wage; therefore we can pay them more. We need creative writers. They cannot do their work without more leisure than other people have. Therefore we can give them more leisure.

Here too there is more cultural determination than there appears to be. Would we need as many doctors as we do if we led healthier lives, or if we were less concerned about our health? If we took money less seriously, would we have to pay so much to get people to be doctors? If our literary tastes were different, would we need so many writers, or would they need so much leisure? In the light of these questions, I cannot find that Rawls' doctrine offers, any more than the others do, a culturally neutral principle for evaluating the inequalities within a culture.

Inequality, then, is a cultural phenomenon, nothing more. Neither the inequalities we have nor any others we can put in their place can be supported under any general philosophical or theological principle. But the fact that inequalities are cultural phenomena does not make them intrinsically unjust. I outlined earlier the things I think everyone must have from society if he is to live a fully human life. If he has them, I cannot see where he has ground for complaint because someone else has them in a different form. We come into life with time and space coordinates; we would be badly disoriented did we not. Our situation in space and time limits the range of options available to us. This is not unjust if the options we have are sufficient to offer us lives worthy of human beings. To say otherwise would require us to say very peculiar things. It would not be enough to say that a farm boy and a city boy were entitled to equal opportunities to make money. We would have to say that they were entitled to equal opportunities to ride escalators, play stickball, milk cows or go trout fishing. We would even have to say that both were entitled to as many lion skins as a Masai, or the same opportunity to spear seals as an Eskimo. These cultural amenities cannot be resolved into money equivalents in order to equalize them, for money is as much a cultural amenity as they are.

If I have resorted to a *reductio ad absurdum* to make my point, it is because it is only at this abstract level that the point can be successfully made. While inequalities are not intrinsically unjust, they are often extrinsically unjust; that is, they often take a form within a particular culture that leads to unjust results. In the first place, they are often structured in such a way as to belie the principle that people are of equal ultimate worth. If having something another person lacks leads you to suppose that you are better than he is, you are very wrong, and a society that encourages you to suppose that is based on a lie. For this reason, I think a society that takes seriously either the Horatio Alger hard work myth or the meritocracy myth is far more pernicious than one where it is well recognized that blind chance or frivolity is the basis of differences.

Inequality, if it is severe enough, tends to erode the sense of community. Disraeli makes this point forcefully with his famous remark about "two nations." Experience of the same kind of thing gives Marx a basis for his theory of inherently antagonistic social classes. Particularly in a society as unstructured and as materialistic as ours, people have to have roughly equivalent material amenities if they are to keep up social relations with one another.

Finally, to the very large extent that society determines what constitutes the good life, it is apt to determine it in terms of ways only a fraction of the society can afford to live. Anyone who falls far enough below the norm thus determined will lack access to what is socially determined to be the good life, and will therefore suffer injustice. In our society, anyone who could not come by a television set would be in this case.

My parting thought on equality is this. It has an important part to play in the pursuit of justice through law, and probably a more important part in this society than in some others (does it enter into the American *Volksgeist*?). But it is neither a sufficient philosophical *a priori* nor a practical panacea, as some writers have supposed it to be. The real demands of justice are neither so superficial nor so neat.

The Principle of Pluralism. The Declaration of the Rights of Man, adopted in the earlier stages of the French Revolution, states that "No person and no body of persons can exercise any authority that does not emanate expressly from the nation." For those who felt oppressed by the moribund medieval patchwork of collectivities and private jurisdictions, this formula no doubt appeared liberating. But to people involved in organizations that actually met their needs and desires it seemed an interference with freedom. As the revolutionary excitement died down, an older theory began to come back into its own, a theory that the state must deal with social groupings not all of its own creation, and that often an individual's freedom can best be exercised through his participation in free groups. Churchmen were the first to appreciate the point, followed by the organizers of labor unions. The German legal scholar Otto von Gierke, the Anglican religious J. N. Figgis, and the Fabian economist Harold Laski were all involved in the revival. The old doctrine in its modern form generally goes by the name of pluralism.

In legal theory pluralism is associated with the realist theory of corporate personality. The law treats corporations and other organized groups for some purposes as if they were individuals. General Motors owns this building and must pay taxes on it. The City of South Bend is liable to a pedestrian who tripped on a hole in the sidewalk. Local 256 of the Teamsters has made a contract with the Acme Trucking Company. The Office of Economic Opportunity has arranged with the Blackstone Rangers to administer a program of job training on the South Side of Chicago. The people who believe that all authority must emanate from the nation tend to believe that all these statements refer to fictitious entities made up by the sovereign for convenience in administering the law. Theirs is called the fiction theory of corporate personality. By contrast, the realist theory holds that business organizations, unions, street gangs, and other groups exist and reach collective decisions without any help from the law, and that the law merely takes them into account as it does the rest of reality. Actually, our law gives some recognition to both these theories: some aspects of corporate personality it bestows, others it merely recognizes. Thus a business organization can have the attributes of a partnership simply by existing, whereas it cannot have those of a corporation without a grant from the state.

The theoretical recognition that groups have a real existence supports a practical recognition of group interests. Recognitions of this kind have been strongly supported by the shift of emphasis in the civil rights movement from concern with individual black people to concern with the black community. Other ethnic groups have begun organizing to press their concerns as have occupational groups and neighborhoods. We discern legally cognizable interests in these groups as fast as they develop spokesmen to present them. We are also beginning to recognize groups such as conservation societies that come together to represent particular aspects of the common good. Such groups have always existed, but the recognition that they have corporate claims to assert is new. We are now on the point of letting them appear in court on behalf of their several concerns.

Our understanding of constitutional freedoms has undergone a similar development. The famous *Kedroff* case (1952) established that freedom of religion required allowing a church to govern itself according to its own constitutional norms. Later cases established a general freedom of association, a right of individuals to associate for lawful purposes, and a collateral right of their associations to operate without unreasonable interference.

Despite our acceptance of pluralism as a doctrine, we do not generally think of social groups as playing a large part in our lives. With the dominance of individualist thought in the nineteenth century, and the rapid social mobility people have experienced in the twentieth, individuals in our society tend to feel more on their own than they did in earlier times or than they do in other societies. Even so, most people will find important autonomous groups in their lives if they look.

The most pervasive example is the nuclear family. It is having its hard knocks these days, but most people still belong to one. The law has always accorded the family a considerable measure of autonomy, generally by leaving the members alone while they settle their own affairs. The reluctance of police to interfere in family fights is proverbial. There are also important limitations on civil suits between the members, tempered these days, to be sure, in cases where the defendant is covered by insurance.

Until quite recently a concomitant of this internal autonomy was the recognition of one person, the husband and father, as representing the family unit before the outside world, signing the papers, paying the bills. A wife has had power since the mid-nineteenth century to administer her own property in her own name, but there is still a tendency for the family property to accumulate in the husband's name. The drive for equal rights for women will probably make considerable changes in these aspects of the law.

It may also produce more general social changes, of which the law will have to take account in due course. If these changes go far enough, they will affect the whole way in which society meets the needs of externalization and accomplishment I described earlier. It has been usual for women to meet these needs within the family, men within the wider society. I cannot see that there is any objection to this differentiation of roles as long as it does meet the needs; nor can I see any objection to meeting the needs instead in some other way. There is probably some natural differentiation of roles between sexes, but it is hard to see it as a matter of whether women make money or not. In any event, the changes proposed at the moment are not all that radical. They seem aimed less at emancipating all women from their traditional roles than at emancipating middle-class women from the roles of domestic servants: roles they took on when the supply of servants gave out after the Second World War. The middle-class pattern of the 1950s where a woman scrubs floors and irons shirts while her husband sits behind a desk thinking deep thoughts and ordering people around, strikes me as neither traditional nor seemly.

A problem the law encounters in dealing with families is the classification of illicit or unconventional arrangements. If two married couples occupy a house and share a common kitchen and table, do they comply with a zoning requirement of one-family occupancy? How about four unmarried students? Does it matter if they are of the same or of different sexes? A woman finds an abandoned child on the street and brings him up. Is she a dependent parent within the meaning of a Workmen's Compensation Law? Widow's benefits under Social Security are cut off on remarriage. A widow begins living with Mr. Jones and calls herself

Mrs. Jones. Does she lose her benefits? There are all kinds of questions like these.

The cohabitation rule under the British Supplementary Benefits (i.e., welfare) Law is an instructive example of how the law can flounder before such questions. The allowance provided under the law for a married couple is less than twice the allowance for a single person. If a couple could get the higher sum by simply omitting a ceremony, the law would be putting a premium on living in sin. Hence, it is provided that if a man and woman cohabit "as man and wife" they can have no more than the couple's allowance, whether they are married or not. But living in the same house does not by itself constitute cohabiting as man and wife; neither does an intermittent sexual relation. Accordingly, the question cannot be determined without a meticulous examination of the couple's whole manner of living: a considerable inroad upon the dignity of the individual.

It seems to me the mischief here is due to the erosion of the idea of the household or the extended family. It was not so long ago that a household might consist of a man, his wife, their children, assorted aunts and uncles, servants, and one or two friends on a long visit. As long as they shared a table and sitting rooms and the like, they could be considered a single unit; sex did not have to enter the picture. The idea, if it could be revived, would be useful for all kinds of groups and communes today.

An extended family includes grandparents, brothers, and sometimes cousins, whether or not they live in the same house. The institution has never had much scope in Anglo-American law. Other systems, though, have given it a considerable formal structure, have assigned it such functions as providing for the guardianship of orphaned relatives, and have even given it an undivided interest in all the ancestral property. About the only function we give it is a modest and moribund part in relieving the poor. Statutes in a number of states require children, grandchildren, parents, brothers and sisters "of sufficient ability" to contribute toward the support of a poor person. Often, the statute is conceived as enacted for the protection of the taxpayer, not of the poor person himself; thus, if Susie does not support Grandma, the authorities can sue her, but Grandma cannot. Often, the statutes are allowed to become a dead letter, because suing the responsible relatives and overcoming the excuses in court is more trouble than it is worth. Of course, many people support their relatives without being sued, but it is not clear how our society currently feels about the responsibility for such support. Consider which of the following sentiments would be yours:

1. It is outrageous that Grandma should have to go on welfare when Susie has enough money to support her.
2. It is outrageous that Grandma's welfare payments should be so low that Susie has to keep sending her money.

(2) seems to be gaining ground these days over (1). If it finally prevails, there will not be much left of the extended family in our law.

Another important group for many people is the subculture, religious (e.g., the Amish), ethnic, or social. The development of pluralism has greatly moderated our enthusiasm for drawing these groups into the mainstream. Efforts to do so are considered violations of religious freedom if the group concerned is religious, cultural genocide if it is ethnic, or conformism if it is social. Generally, the legal arrangements for protecting individual freedom are adequate to support legitimate subcultures (i.e., those that do not require behavior that would not be tolerated in individuals) for anyone desiring to participate. Most of the legal problems involve passing on the subculture to another generation. Bringing up children necessarily involves a certain measure of coercion; hence, a child brought up in the subculture is to some extent forcibly excluded from the mainstream, and vice versa. This fact produces a number of puzzling conflicts: many of those over parental fitness in the divorce and juvenile courts, or over anything from language teaching to vaccination in the schools.

In recent years the sharpest conflict of this kind has been the one over the refusal of the Old Order Amish to send their children to high school. They believe that high schol prepares children for life in the world (i.e., the mainstream) and encourages them to opt for that life. If that is the case, then not attending will restrict children's options, and tend to force them into the subculture. For this reason, the Amish have failed to convince some of the chief proponents of religious freedom (e.g., the American Civil Liberties Union and Mr. Justice Douglas) that their cause is worthy of support. The Supreme Court, however, has recently ruled in their favor, on what seem like pragmatic rather than philosophical grounds: the Amish are nice people, and high school is not all that important. To my mind, this is the right way to go about it. Group interests, like individual interests, are not to be evaluated in the abstract, but in terms of their contribution to the welfare of real human beings. In such an evaluation, the advantage of being brought up in a cohesive and self-confident subculture is not to be overlooked.

The groups that are most fruitful in legal problems are membership corporations and unincorporated associations. These can be organized for almost any purpose. One is distinguishable from the other only in juridical form. Churches are usually incorporated; labor unions not; trade associations and the like about half and half. In either case, you become affiliated by signing up and paying your dues, and governance is provided by elected representatives of the members. A member has a property right in the common funds; hence, he cannot be expelled without a legitimate reason and a fair procedure.

These associations, if strategically placed and left to their own devices, can have a drastic effect on the affairs of members and nonmembers alike. A union may fix your wages, or even determine whether you have a job. A trade association may pool information and services so effectively that nonmembers cannot compete with members. A county medical society may determine which doctors may admit their patients to the local hospital. An organization for cancer research may tap the sources of financial support so well that no one else can get money for a project in the area.

The law can work either to curb the power of associations or to control it so it will serve legitimate purposes. To the extent that pluralism has replaced individualism in our thinking, the former course has tended to give way to the latter. Thus, in less than a century, our attitude toward labor unions has gone from hostility to neutrality to support to regulation. In the case of trade and professional associations, we have vacillated between restricting them, usually under the antitrust laws, and letting them alone. But we are beginning to allow them a broader scope under a more active supervision.

The issues are numerous, and reflect the incomplete evolution of our thinking. Do we permit the closed shop contract, whereby you have to belong to the union to get a job, or the union shop contract, whereby you have to join the union after you are hired, or do we enact right to work legislation that protects you against being made to join a union at all? (Generally, we opt for the union shop.) If not belonging to the union will adversely affect your chance for a job, what recourse do you have if the union will not let you join? (If they do not have a good reason for excluding you, the courts will usually make them admit you.) Can the union require you to support particular stands on the issues of the day? (No, your constitutional rights are good against the union as they are against the government.) Suppose an employer wants to deal with a union that the majority of his employees do not want? (Except in agriculture, which is not covered by the applicable legislation, the employer must bargain with the union chosen by the majority of his employees: the agriculture exception is responsible for the lettuce boycott.) Can a trade association tell you how to run your business? (It can lay down ethical standards for improving the trade, but cannot fix prices; other matters are unresolved.) Can it arbitrarily exclude a person in the trade from joining? (No.)

In all these matters, the approach toward which we seem to be moving is this: If a group has a proper common good, it is appropriate, and probably desirable, that they should organize to enhance it. But the organization they develop for the purpose must be open on fair terms to anyone who is entitled to participate in that common good. They may not impinge on individuals more than is necessary to secure their common good, or more than their particular common good deserves. The law will control them to maintain these limits, to enforce the interests of other individuals and groups, and to protect the common good of the wider community.

The development of this kind of pluralism is eminently desirable, but a note of caution is still in order. The fundamental tension between the individual and the group is not eliminated by bringing the group closer to home. To illustrate, here is a case, one of rather frequent occurrence, which offers considerable danger of going astray. An employer negotiates with the union representing his employees a contract whereby certain classes of workers are laid off, retired, or sent on vacation without pay. Pursuant to the contract, a certain employee is put out of his job. He applies for unemployment compensation under a statute that denies it if he has "voluntarily" quit work. The question is whether the fact that his leaving was pursuant to a contract made, in fact insisted on, by his representative makes it voluntary. The courts that have considered the question have split about half and half. But there is no doubt in my mind that the employee should prevail. The fact that the union represents, and rightly, a common good in which he participates does not mean that it represents him as a human being.

CONCLUSION

Jean-Paul Sartre says hell is other people. Sir Thomas Browne says we are beholden to every man we meet that he does not kill us. Saint John says we have passed from death into life because we love the brethren. Man's encounter with his neighbor is both death and life to him. We encounter one another within the ongoing life of the community, among the subordinate groups that make it up, and in the presence of the economic, social, political, and historical forces it sets in motion. We thread our way through this profusion of forces and collectivities with the hope, or if not the hope, the demand — in a word, the expectation — that our encounter with our neighbor will be for life and not for death. To pursue justice is above all else to give this expectation a voice.

We may think of the legal enterprise as participating in the divine power of voicing expectations from the mountain and hurling thunderbolts in their support, but the work is more often done in offices and libraries, or in legislative and judicial halls of less than Sinaitic proportions. The task not only of the practicing lawyer, but of the judge, the legislator, and the administrator as well, is to guide the citizen in living up to the reasonable expectations of his neighbors and to support him in claiming fulfillment for his own. In a complex society (and all societies are in one way or another complex) marked by forces and developments but dimly understood and but tenuously controlled, it takes learning and sophistication to do what has to be done. But compassion and dedication are more important still. If the legal enterprise is to speak with a divine voice, it must reflect the presence of the redemptive Word who is named both Counselor and Advocate. It has long been the boast of our own legal system that it is the product not of philosophers or planners, but of practicing lawyers — that is, of counselors and advocates. May it long continue to be.

NOTES AND REFERENCES

Preface

p xi

The French tag is from Musset's Preface to a collection of his works (1840).

Chapter 2

pp. 15–16

The Supreme Court case on Dorr's affair is *Luther* v. *Borden*, 7 How. 1 (U. S., 1849). The treason trial is *State* v. *Dorr*, 2 Am. St. Trials 69. A compendium of other material on the subject is *Report on Affairs in Rhode Island*, House Rep. No. 546, 28th Cong. 1st Sess. (1844).

pp. 16–17

On the replacement of state constitutions, see *In re Opinion to the Governor*, 55 R. I. 56, 178 Atl. 433 (1935); *Wheeler* v. *Board of Trustees*, 200 Ga. 323, 37 S. E. 2d 322 (1946).

p. 17

The Commonwealth cases on the legitimacy of post-coup governments are all cited in *Madzinbamuto* v. *Lardner-Burke*, [1968] All E. R. 561 (P. C.), affirming the Rhodesia case.

The Articles of Impeachment against Richard II are in *Rot. Parl.* iii, 421a. The Supreme Court's one-man-one-vote line begins with *Baker* v. *Carr*, 369 U. S. 186 (1962), and reaches its ideological apogee with *Reynolds* v. *Sims*, 377 U. S. 533 (1964), and the four following cases in the same volume. See the dissenting opinion of Stewart, J., *Lucas* v. *General Assembly*, 377 U. S. 713, 744, applicable to the lot.

Hale's rationale for accepting office under the Commonwealth is in Campbell, *Lives of the Chief Justices* i, 527–28 (1849). For the attitude of German courts toward Nazi legislation, see H. Rommen, "Natural Law in Decisions of the Federal Supreme Court and of the Constitutional Courts in Germany, *Nat. L. Forum* iv, 1, 15–16 (1959).

p. 19

The case holding that Americans are entitled to juries in criminal cases is *Duncan* v. *Louisiana*, 391 U. S. 145 (1968).

p. 24

The Holmes quote about general propositions is from his dissenting opinion in *Lochner* v. *New York*, 198 U. S. 45, 76 (1905).

pp. 25–29

The classic workmen's compensation fight case is *Hartford Accident & Indemnity Co.* v. *Cardillo*, 112 F. 2d 11 (D. C. Cir. 1940) (decision for employee). The horseplay cases are numerous. *Ognibene* v. *Rochester Mfg. Co.*, 298 N. Y. 85, 80 N. E. 2d 749 (1948) is typical. Judge

Fuld, for the majority, denied compensation to the instigator. I find Judge Desmond's dissenting opinion more persuasive. Cases in other jurisdictions are split. The head-in-dumbwaiter case is *Bethlehem Steel Co.* v. *Parker*, 64 F. Supp. 615 (D. Md. 1946).

pp. 27-28

Dworkin's analysis of rules and principles is in "The Model of Rules," *U. Chi. L. Rev.* xxxv, 14 (1967).

Chapter 3

pp. 33-34

The cases on making motorcyclists wear helmets are collected in an Annotation, 32 A. L. R. 3d 1270 (1970). I see from the British papers that I had forgotten the Sikhs when I said there was no one to characterize the nonwearing of helmets as a matter of conscience. But let the point stand with them as an exception.

pp. 36-37

Pueblo v. *Tribunal Superior* is reported in *Revista Juridica de la Universidad de Puerto Rico*, xxxvi, 393 (1966). *Duncan* v. *Louisiana* is cited above (c. 2). The *Dred Scott* case is *Dred Scott* v. *Sandford*, 19 How. 393 (U. S., 1857). The Maryland case referred to in the same connection is *Horace Mann League* v. *Board of Public Works*, 242 Md. 645, 220 A. 2d 51 (1966). The Holmes quotation is from *Missouri* v. *Holland*, 252 U. S. 416, 433-34 (1920).

pp. 40-41

The case of the demagogue arrested by the police is *Terminiello* v. *Chicago*, 337 U. S. 1 (1949). The shopping center case is *Schwartz-Torrance Inv. Corp.* v. *Bakery & Con. Wkrs. Union*, 61 Cal. 2d 766, 394 P. 2d 921 (1964). I am indebted for this citation to Prof. Joseph C. Smith of the Faculty of Law of the University of British Columbia. His *Readings in Jurisprudence* 2 ed., (University of British Columbia, 1969), pp. 4-15 include this case, and, by way of contrast, a couple of Canadian cases that approach the same problem in a more conceptual way. *Grosvenor Park Shopping Center Ltd.* v. *Waloshin*, 46 D.L.R. 2d 750 (Sask. 1964); *Zeller's (Western) Ltd.* v. *Retail Food and Drug Clerks Union*, 36 D.L.R. 2d 581 (B. C. 1963); Ibid., 42 D.L.R. 2d 582 (B. C. 1964).

p. 43

Cowan's doctrine of social security interests is set forth in "The Impact of Social Security on the Philosophy of Law," *Rutgers L. Rev.* xi, 688 (1957).

pp. 43-44

The eponymous Brandeis brief was used in *Muller* v. *Oregon*, 208 U. S. 412 (1908). The Oklahoma ice case was *New State Ice Co.* v. *Liebmann*, 285 U. S. 262 (1932). For a recent use of empirical data in criminal procedure, see *In re Gault*, 387 U. S. 1 (1967), establishing procedural standards for juvenile courts. Cahn's objections to the use of data in civil rights cases are in "Jurisprudence," *Annual Survey of American Law, 1954*, N. Y. U. L. Rev. xxx, 150 (1955). For an elaboration of my views on the use of data, see "Due Process and Social Legislation in the Supreme Court," *Notre Dame Lawyer* xxxiii, 5 (1957).

p. 46

"Fashion into one united people. . . ." is from a prayer for our country in the American Book of Common Prayer.

Chapter 4

p. 61

There is material on the responsibility of relatives under Old Age Assistance laws in *Social Welfare and the Individual—Cases and Materials*, Levy, Lewis, and Martin, eds., (Foundation Press, 1971) 121-29.

The material from *Doctor and Student* is in Dialogue I, Chapter XXI.

pp. 65-67

My view about penal laws owes a great deal to T. E. Davitt, *The Nature of Law* (Herder, 1951).

You can probably find at least as much as you care to know about the Indiana gambling laws in *Tinder* v. *Music Operating, Inc.*, 237 Ind. 33, 142 N.E. 2d 610 (1957). We are unique in that our turkey raffles are held in disregard of our constitution as well as our laws. Ind. Const. Art. 15, Sec. 8.

Our almost totally ignored Sunday law is Ind. Code 35-1-86-1.

Chapter 5

pp. 71-72

The Canadian Bill of Rights is 8-9 Eliz. 2, c. 44 (1960). The most important case applying it is *Regina* v. *Drybones*, 9 D.L.R. 3d 473 (1969).

p. 73

Of the various consequences I envisaged from legalizing prostitution, one has already materialized. A man recently complained to the civil rights commission in Nevada concerning race discrimination at a brothel. I have lost the reference, but it appeared that the commission was routinely processing his complaint.

pp. 73-74

For an elaboration of my point about a society's laws giving symbolic content to its aspirations, see my "A Prospectus for a Symbolist Jurisprudence," *Nat. L. Forum*, ii, 88 (1957).

p. 75

The case holding laws against contraceptives unconstitutional is *Griswold* v. *Connecticut*, 381 U. S. 479 (1965). Llewellyn's example of the elimination of library pilferage is in "Law Observance versus Law Enforcement," *Jurisprudence* 399, 408 (Chicago, 1962). The material from the Theodosian Code on runaway municipal officials is bk. XII, title 1 passim. On the cry of Haro, see "Haro, Clameur de," Ency. Brit., 14th ed., or "Harrow," *O.E.D.*, Pharr ed. (Princeton, 1952).

Chapter 6

pp. 93-94

For the practical applications referred to in my introduction of the right-remedy problem, see *Vaca* v. *Sipes,* 386 U. S. 171 (1967) (union member limited to grievance procedure unless union acts wrongfully in refusing to process grievance); *Kesler* v. *Utah Dept. of Public Safety,* 369 U. S. 153 (1962) (state can suspend license of bankrupt for not paying judgment in automobile case); *Wightman* v. *Wightman,* 4 Johns. Ch. 343 (N. Y., 1820) (abolition of jurisdiction of English ecclesiastical courts in America gives New York Chancery court jurisdiction to annul a marriage—per Kent, C.); *Home Building & Loan Ass'n.* v. *Blaisdell,* 290 U. S. 398 (1934) (upholding state mortgage moratorium act).

p. 96

The habeas corpus case in which the wife was released from her husband's custody is *Regina* v. *Jackson,* [1891] 1 Q. B. 671 (C. A.), discussed in Chapter 8, *infra.*

p. 99

Ashby v. *White* is reported in 2 Ld. Raym. 938, 92 Eng. Rep. 126 (1704). In the same connection, see the provision in the Statute of Westminster II, 13 Edw. 1, St. 1, c. 24 (1285), giving a remedy in any case *like* a case where there is already a remedy. *Devereux* v. *Tuchet,* Selden Soc., xx, 16, 19 (1310) *Stirkeland* v. *Brunolfshead,* Id., 106, 109 (1310) show the development of the writ of entry *in consimili casu* in response to this principle.

pp. 100-101

The case holding that charging unreasonable prices cannot be made a crime is *United States* v. *Cohen Grocery Co.,* 255 U. S. 81 (1921). Holding the same as to being a "member of a gang" is *Lanzetta* v. *New Jersey,* 306 U. S. 451 (1939). The case of the animal or obstruction on the railroad track is *Nashville and Knoxville R. R.* v. *Davis,* 78 S.W. 1050 (Tenn. 1902).

pp. 102-104

The quote from Cardozo is in *Schechter Corp.* v. *United States,* 295 U. S. 495, 551 (1935).

The Supreme Court's decisions on health inspectors are *Camara* v. *Municipal Court,* 387 U. S. 523 (1967) and *See* v. *Seattle,* 387 U. S. 541 (1967). On forbidding margarine, see *Powell* v. *Pennsylvania,* 127 U. S. 678 (1888). Another example of a law which forbids something innocuous because of the difficulty of proving something harmful is Section 16(b) of the Securities Exchange Act of 1934. See *Smolowe* v. *Delendo Corp.,* 136 F. 2d 231 (2d Cir. 1943).

pp. 104-105

The age-old practice of repossessing merchandise without a prior hearing was declared unconstitutional in *Fuentes* v. *Shevia,* 407 U. S. 67 (1972).

p. 108

The leading case on whether occasional sexual lapses vitiate the "good moral character" required for naturalization is *Schmidt* v. *United States,* 177 F. 2d 450 (2d. Cir. 1949).

p. 109

The decision as to the remedy for school segregation is *Brown* v. *Board of Education,* 347 U. S. 294 (1955). Note that the Supreme Court actually modified a decision of the Supreme Court of Delaware ordering immediate admission of the plaintiffs. *Gebhard* v. *Belton,* 33 Del. Ch. 144, 91 A. 2d 137 (1952); cf. *Simmons* v. *Steiner,* 49 Del. 75, 111 A. 2d 574 (1955). For examples of the treatment of buses, labor unions, parks, and universities, see, respectively, *Morgan* v. *Virginia,* 328 U. S. 373 (1946); *Steele* v. *Louisville and Nashville R. R.,* 323 U. S. 192 (1944); *Watson* v. *Memphis,* 373 U. S. 526 (1963); *Hawkins* v. *Board of Control,* 350 U. S. 413 (1956).

pp. 112-13

To the effect that no standards are necessary in delegating rule-making authority to the agency regulating the airport, see *Commonwealth* v. *Diaz,* 326 Mass. 525, 95 N.E. 2d 666 (1950).

Chapter 7

p. 121

My views on Ellul are developed in a Book Review in *Nat. L. Forum,* viii, 188 (1963).

pp. 123-25

Dora Jones' case is *United States* v. *Ingalls,* 73 F. Supp. 76 (S. D. Cal. 1947). The case of the workmen's compensation claimant who went into the alley for a smoke is *Bradford's Case,* 319 Mass. 621, 67 N.E. 2d 149 (1946); that of the one who stopped to render assistance at an accident is *Puttkammer* v. *Industrial Commission,* 371 Ill. 497, 21 N.E. 2d 575 (1939). The stomach-pumping case is *Rochin* v. *California,* 342 U. S. 165 (1952); the blood sample case is *Schmerber* v. *California,* 384 U. S. 757 (1966). The case of the spring gun in the watermelon patch is *State* v. *Childers,* 133 Ohio St. 508, 14 N.E. 2d 767 (1938).

pp. 125-26

The quote from Pollock and Maitland is *History of English Law,* ii, 2 ed., 474. You can learn all about deodands from the material in *Bacon's New Abridgment,* ii, (London, 1832) 632-34. They were abolished by 9-10 Vic. c. 62 (1846). I cannot remember where I read that the statute was occasioned by the forefeiture of a locomotive, but it is too good a story to leave out.

p. 127

The quote about workmen's compensation laws is from *New York Central R. R.* v. *White,* 243 U. S. 188, 205 (1917). The fellow servant doctrine was established by Massachusetts' great Chief Justice Shaw in *Farwell* v. *Boston & Worcester R. R.,* 4 Metc. 49 (Mass. 1842). It is interesting that the doctrine developed quite independently on both sides of the Atlantic at about the same time. *Priestley* v. *Fowler,* 3 M. & W. 1, 150 Eng. Rep. 1030 (Exch. 1837).

pp. 128-29

Ewing v. *Black* is 172 F. 2d 331 (6th Cir. 1949); *Solow* v. *General Motors Truck Co.* is 64 F. 2d 105 (2d Cir. 1933). The leading blasting case is *Exner* v. *Sherman Power Const. Co.,* 54 F. 2d 510 (2d Cir. 1931).

p. 132

On shooting the man who comes after you with a knife, see *Brown* v. *United States,* 256 U. S. 335 (1921), and Mr. Justice Holmes's famous statement that "Detached reflection cannot be demanded in the presence of an uplifted knife." Id. at 343. On walking on the wrong side of the road, see *Tedla* v. *Ellman*, 280 N. Y. 124, 19 N. E. 2d 987 (1939).

p. 133

An example of a snake-handling case is *Harden* v. *State*, 188 Tenn. 17, 216 S.W. 2d 708 (1949). Such cases all hark back to *Reynolds* v. *United States*, 98 U. S. 145 (1879), upholding the suppression of polygamy in Utah. The other work of mine referred to in this connection is "Sub Deo et Lege: A Study of Free Exercise," *Religion and the Public Order* iv, 3 (1966). The case upholding the right of the Amish parent to keep his child out of high school is *Wisconsin* v. *Yoder*, 406 U. S. 205 (1972).

p. 134

There are many cases involving parents who go in for faith healing. *Bradley* v. *State*, 79 Fla, 651, 84 So. 677 (1920) gives a good idea of how the courts deal with them. The Supreme Court's broadening of the concept of religion for purposes of applying the conscientious objector exemption is in *United States* v. *Seeger*, 380 U. S. 163 (1965).

p. 135

On entrapment, see *Sherman* v. *United States*, 356 U. S. 369 (1958). *Pike* v. *Pike* is 100 N. J. Eq. 486, 136 Atl. 421 (Ch. 1927). On workmen's compensation for suicides, see *Barber* v. *Industrial Comm'n*, 241 Wis. 462, 6 N. W. 2d 199 (1942); Larson, *Workmen's Compensation Law* §36.

p. 136

The classic case on the right to live down old scandals is *Melvin* v. *Reid*, 112 Cal. App. 285, 297 Pac. 91 (1931). It has probably been eroded a good deal by the Surpeme Court's freedom-of-the-press decision in *Time Inc.* v. *Hill*, 385 U. S. 374 (1967), but one can still hope it retains some validity. Prosser, *Law of Torts*, 4 ed., (1971) 828. The leading case on the rights of illegitimate children is *Levy* v. *Louisiana*, 391 U. S. 68 (1968); that on welfare for unmarried mothers is *King* v. *Smith*, 392 U. S. 309 (1968). *Kendall* v. *Housing Authority*, 196 Md. 370, 76 A. 2d 767 (1950) is a major case for compensating a woman for the death of the man who supported her. An example familiar to most law students of a court coping with property problems when a liaison breaks up is *Tami* v. *Pikowitz*, 138 N. J. Eq. 410, 48 A. 2d 221 (1946), a rhetorical tour de force by Wilfred Jayne, one of our foremost judicial humorists, as well as a wise and compassionate judge.

The limited constitutional protection afforded to commercial advertising was established in *Valentine* v. *Chrestensen*, 316 U. S. 52 (1942), and has not been seriously questioned since. The obscenity cases are in a state of flux. The latest Supreme Court statement at this point (May, 1974), is *Paris Adult Theatre I* v. *Slaton*, 413 U. S. 49 (1973).

pp. 137-38

The idea of having doors to open is movingly developed by Dorothy Donnelly in *The Golden Well*, (London, 1950) 73-89. The case of the doctor and his curious friend is *De May* v. *Roberts*, 46 Mich. 160,

9 N. W. 146 (1881). *State* v. *Long*, 93 N. C. 542 (1885) is the case of the woman who offered to submit to her would-be ravisher for ten cents. The cigarette burner's case was *Commonwealth* v. *Farrell*, 322 Mass. 606, 78 N. E. 2d 697 (1948), that of the flagellator *Rex* v. *Donovan*, [1934] 2 K.B. 498 (C.A.). On tooth transplants, see Taylor, *History of Dentistry* 70 and passim (Philadelphia, 1922).

The Warren and Brandeis article is "The Right to Privacy," *Harv. L. Rev.* iv, 193 (1890). The case of the creditor who put the sign in his store window is *Brents* v. *Morgan*, 211 Ky. 765, 299 S. W. 967, 55 A.L.R. 964 (1927); that of the landlord who bugged the tenant's bedroom is *Hamberger* v. *Eastman*, 106 N. H. 107, 206 A. 2d 239 (1964). *Griswold* v. *Connecticut*, 381 U. S. 479 (1965), the contraception case, is discussed in Chapter 5. *Roe* v. *Wade*, 410 U. S. 113 (1973) is the abortion case. On gratuitous publicity, see *Melvin* v. *Reid* and *Time Inc.* v. *Hill*, *supra*, note to p. 136.

p. 139

The case of the man who cut his throat in the kitchen is *Blakeley* v. *Shortal's Estate*, 236 Iowa 787, 20 N.W. 2d 28 (1945). On harrassment in general, see *Flamm* v. *Van Nierop*, 56 Misc. 2d 1059, 291 N.Y.S. 2d 189 (Sup. 1968), and on bill collectors in particular, Berger, "The Bill Collector and the Law," *De Paul L. Rev.* xvii, 327 (1968). *Price* v. *Yellow Pine Paper Mill Co.*, 240 S.W. 588 (Tex. Civ. App. 1922) is the case of the woman whose husband was brought home covered with blood. On the mother whose child is run over the leading English case, *Hambrook* v. *Stokes Bros.*, (1952) 1 K.B. 141 (C.A.), was in her favor, while the leading American case, *Waube* v. *Warrington*, 216 Wis. 603, 258 N.W. 497 (1935) was against her. Since *Dillon* v. *Legg*, 68 Cal. 2d 728, 441 P. 2d 912 (1968), the American courts have begun taking a new look at the question, with varying results.

Chapter 8

pp. 141-43

The Chesterton quote is one of a set of epigraphs in *The Law in Literature*, Vol. 1 (London, 1960). I have not been able to run down the original source. *Local Government Board* v. *Arlidge* is [1915] A.C. 120. The crucial holding in *Morgan* is found in *Morgan* v. *United States*, 298 U. S. 468, 481-82 (1936). Judge Frank's endorsement of the special verdict as the next best thing to abolishing civil juries entirely is found in *Skidmore* v. *Baltimore & Ohio R. R.*, 167 F. 2d 54 (2d Cir. 1948). On the need for personal encounter in the administrative process, see *Goldberg* v. *Kelly*, 397 U. S. 254 (1970).

pp. 144-45

The provision of Magna Carta about marriages is Art. 6: "Heirs shall be married without disparagement. . . ." The case denying compensation to a marriage broker is *Hall* v. *Potter*, Show. P.C. 76, 1 Eng. Rep. 52 (H.L. 1695). Applying the same rule to parents are *Keat* v. *Allen*, 2 Vern. 588, 33 Eng. Rep. 983 (Ch. 1707); *Duke of Hamilton* v. *Mohun*, 1 P. Wms. 118, 24 Eng. Rep. 319 (Ch. 1710). On inducing breach of a marriage contract, see *Conway* v. *O'Brien*, 269 Mass. 425, 169 N. E. 491, 73 A.L.R. 1448 (1929).

Merrill v. *Peaslee* is 146 Mass. 460, 16 N. E. 271 (1888). Its teaching has not won universal acceptance. Anno., 149 A.L.R. 1016 (1944). *Perez* v. *Lippold* is 32 Cal. 2d 711, 198 P. 2d 17 (1948). The lines of poetry are from Part V of *The Waste Land.*

p. 146

The quote from the *De Amore* is from the Seventh Dialogue, between a man of the higher nobility and a woman of the simple nobility, *The Art of Courtly Love,* Parry tr. (New York, 1941).

p. 147

The case of E. H. Jackson, who carried his wife off, is *Regina* v. *Jackson,* [1891] 1 Q.B. 671 (C.A.); that of Mrs. Nanda, who tried to disrupt her husband's life with his mistress is *Nanda* v. *Nanda,* [1967] 3 All E.R. 401 (1966).

In *Donnell* v. *Donnell,* 220 Tenn. 169, 415 S.W. 2d 127 (1967), a woman recovered $25,000 against a successful rival for her husband's affections. The plaintiff in *Glatstein* v. *Grund,* 243 Iowa 541, 51 N.W. 2d 162, 36 A.L.R. 2d 531 (1952) recovered $15,000 from her mother-in-law. An injunction against alienating the affections of the plaintiff's husband was upheld in *Logan* v. *Davidson,* 282 Ala. 327, 211 So. 2d 461 (1968), although the leading case on the point, *Snedaker* v. *King,* 111 Ohio St. 225, 145 N.E. 15 (1924) holds injunctive relief inappropriate in these cases. *Hitaffer* v. *Argonne Co.,* 183 F. 2d 811 (D.C. Cir. 1950) is a major case explaining, revising, and extending the action for loss of consortium.

p. 148

For an elaboration of my views on the dynamics of social reform and the role of law in the process, see my review of Maritain's *On the Philosophy of History, Nat. L. Forum,* iii, (1958) 210.

pp. 150-51

The case of Trop, the deserter, is *Trop* v. *Dulles,* 356 U. S. 86 (1958). The quote is from pp. 101-102. The passage from Simone Weil is from *The Need for Roots* (New York, 1952) p. 35.

On the effect of antitrust laws on service station ownership, see *Standard Oil Co. of California* v. *United States,* 337 U. S. 293, 315 (Douglas, J., dissenting).

Cases on the value of second-hand furniture, contributory negligence in leaving things on your land where your neighbor can injure them, and the right of parents to be supported in their own home are, respectively, *Birmingham Ry. Light & Power Co.* v. *Hinton,* 157 Ala. 630, 47 So. 576 (1908); *LeRoy Fibre Co.* v. *Chicago, M. & St. P. Ry.,* 232 U. S. 340 (1914); and *Los Angeles County* v. *LaFuente,* 20 Cal. 2d 870, 129 P. 2d 378 (1942).

pp. 155-56

Wilkie v. *O'Connor* is 261 App. Div. 373, 25 N. Y. S. 2d 617 (4th Dept. 1941). *Adams* v. *Tanner* is 244 U. S. 590 (1917). The habeas corpus proceeding the foster parents lost to the agency is *In re Jewish Child Care Association,* 5 N. Y. 2d 222, 156 N. E. 2d 700 (1959).

pp. 157-59

The statement of the principle of subsidiarity is found in §§ 79-80 of *Quadrigesimo Anno.* On the application of the principle to broadcasting, see *National Broadcasting Co.* v. *United States,* 319 U.S. 190 (1943).

pp. 160-61

Lucas v. General Assembly, 377 U. S. 713 (1964) held that a state
cannot achieve regional balance in its legislature at the expense of equal
representation. On community vetoes of low-cost housing, see James v.
Valtierra, 402 U. S. 137 (1971). San Antonio School District v.
Rodriguez, 411 U. S. 1 (1973) seems to have disposed of local school
financing as a federal constitutional matter; but state constitutional
questions are still open. Serrano v. Priest, 5 Cal. 3d 584, 487 P. 2d
1241, 41 A.L.R. 3d 1187 (1971).

DeFunis v. Odegaard, 416 U. S. 312 (1974) threw out the case involving discrimination in favor of racial minorities. DeFunis, with
qualifications that would have gotten him into the state university had
he been black, was excluded, then admitted pendente lite. By the time
the case was argued in the Supreme Court, he was about to graduate,
rendering the case moot. Lau v. Nichols, 414 U. S. 563 (1974) holds
that a school system is required to do something for students who are
not fluent in English. The case involved Chinese, but it is regarded as a
major victory for Spanish-speaking people. Mills v. Board of Education
of the District of Columbia, 348 F. Supp. 866 (D. D.C. 1972) is an
example of a case requiring special programs for handicapped children.

The compulsory murder case, the cannibalism case, and the case of
throwing people out of the boat are, respectively, Arp v. State, 97 Ala.
5, 12, So. 301 (1893); Regina v. Dudley and Stephens, L.R. 14 Q.B.
273 (1884); United States v. Holmes, Fed. Cas. #15,383 (E.D.Pa.
1842).

p. 163

On money as a cultural amenity, see S. H. Frankel, "Concepts of
Income and Welfare and Intercomparability of National Income Ag-
gregates" in The Economic Impact on Under-Developed Societies,
(Cambridge, Mass. 1955) 28.

p. 165

The two main cases on the standing of associations to appear in
court are Sierra Club v. Morton, 405 U. S. 727 (1972) and United
States v. SCRAP, 412 U. S. 669 (1973). The case on ecclesiastical self-
government is Kedroff v. St. Nicholas Cathedral, 344 U. S. 94 (1952).
In connection with it, see my "The Last Days of Erastianism—Forms in
the American Church-State Nexus," Harv. Theol. Rev., lxii, (1969)
301. The case generally regarded as establishing freedom of association
in this country is National Association for the Advancement of Colored
People v. Alabama, 357 U. S. 449 (1958). The Irish Constitution makes
specific provision for the right to form associations. National Union of
Railwaymen v. Sullivan, [1947] Irish Rep. 77.

pp. 166-67

State v. Rhodes, 61 N.C. 453 (1867) provides an interesting, and
perhaps unique, application of the noninterference doctrine, holding
that while a man has no right to beat his wife, the state should not
interfere unless he beats her too hard. On tort actions between family
members, and the effect of insurance, see Gelbman v. Gelbman, 23
N. Y. 2d 434, 245 N. E. 2d 192 (1969). Cases like Balfour v. Balfour,
[1919] 2 K.B. 571 (C.A.) do not hold that family members cannot sue

one another for breach of contract, but that their arrangements for ordering domestic and financial affairs are not to be treated as contracts.

Department of Agriculture v. *Moreno*, 413 U. S. 528 (1973) held it was unconstitutional to give better food stamp treatment to households whose members were all related than to other households. However, *Village of Belle Terre* v. *Boraas*, 416 U. S. 1 (1974) upheld a zoning rule limiting one-family occupancy to cases where not more than two unrelated persons lived together. *Faber* v. *Industrial Commission*, 352 Ill. 115, 185 N.E. 255 (1933) recognizes the parental status of the woman who takes in the child. On cohabitation as remarriage, see *Elkhorn Coal Corp.* v. *Tackett*, 243 Ky. 694, 49 S.W. 2d 571 (1932), which seems to go off on a presumption of legal marriage from the fact of living together. The problems with the British cohabitation rule are described in T. Lynes, *The Penguin Guide to Supplementary Benefits* (London, 1972) 154-61.

For some of the functions of the extended family in other cultures, see arts. 1091-1137 of the preCommunist Chinese Civil Code, and the material on the Hindu Joint Family in Gledhill, *The Republic of India* (British Commonwealth Law Series, London, 1951) 210-13. I referred above (c. 4) to material on the responsibility of relatives for supporting old people. See also *Wood* v. *Waggoner*, 67 S. D. 365, 293 N. W. 188 (1940), holding that a man who is being voluntarily supported by his son-in-law is not in need within the meaning of the Old Age Assistance Laws.

p. 168-170

For an example of subcultural problems in a child custody suit, see *Application of Auster*, 198 Misc. 1055, 100 N.Y.S. 2d 60, *affirmed* 278 App. Div. 656, 102 N.Y.S. 2d 418, *affirmed* 302 N.Y. 883, 100 N.E. 2d 56, *cert. denied*, 342 U.S. 884 (1951). The Amish high school case, *Wisconsin* v. *Yoder*, 406 U. S. 205 (1972) was mentioned also in c. 4 above. An example of a case compelling a union to admit a would-be member, because a "labor organization could not properly maintain a closed union and a closed shop at the same time" is *Thorman* v. *International Alliance*, 49 Cal. 2d 629, 320 P. 2d 404 (1958). Upholding constitutional rights against union interference is *Spayd* v. *Ringing Rock Lodge*, 270 Pa. 67, 113 Atl. 70 (1921). On the right to belong to trade associations, see *Falcone* v. *Middlesex County Medical Soc.*, 34 N. J. 582, 178 A. 2d 791 (1961).

Two cases on the voluntariness of being laid off pursuant to a union contract are *Bergseth* v. *Zinsmaster Baking Co.*, 252 Minn. 63, 89 N. W. 2d 172 (1958), denying benefits, and *Employment Sec. Comm'n.* v. *Magma Copper Co.*, 90 Ariz. 104, 366 p. 2d 84 (1961), allowing them.

Sartre's famous "l'enfer, c'est les autres" appears at the end of *Huis Clos*. Browne's remark is taken from *Religio Medici* Part I, Sec. 44. The text about passing from death into life is 1 John 3:14.